SAMSUNG GALAXY S24 USER GUIDE

Beginner and Professional Guide to Navigate, Innovate, Elevate Your Path to Smartphone Mastery

BETTY M. ATKINS

Table of Contents

INTRODUCTION

Embark on a transformative journey into the realm of technological excellence with the highly anticipated Samsung Galaxy S24. This flagship marvel goes beyond conventional boundaries, reshaping the smartphone landscape with a harmonious blend of revolutionary features. Immerse yourself in an unparalleled visual experience through the Infinity-O Dynamic AMOLED display, now crisper and more vibrant than ever before. Delve into a seamless dance of fluidity with the mesmerizing 120Hz Pro Motion refresh rate, ensuring every interaction is a display of unparalleled smoothness. Elevate your photography to new heights with the Quad Ultra Vision Camera system, featuring a 108MP main sensor that captures every detail with exquisite clarity. AI-driven enhancements and advanced Night Vision technology transform each snapshot into a masterpiece, unveiling the true potential of mobile photography. Unleash unrivaled performance with the latest Exynos 7nm+ Octa-Core processor, delivering lightning-fast speeds and efficiency that redefine smartphone benchmarks. Seamlessly step into the future with 5G connectivity, ensuring a lag-free and immersive experience whether you're streaming, gaming, or engaging in video conferencing.

Bid farewell to battery anxiety as the intelligent Adaptive Power Saving Mode learns your usage patterns, optimizing power consumption and extending your device's longevity. Crafted with precision, the Galaxy S24 boasts a sleek and ergonomic design, featuring premium build materials and exquisite color options that make a bold style statement, setting you apart in the world of devices. Privacy takes center stage with advanced biometric authentication, combining facial recognition and an ultrasonic fingerprint sensor to create an impenetrable fortress of security. Transform your device into an entertainment powerhouse with Dolby

Atmos audio and an expanded storage capacity, turning the Galaxy S24 into your gateway to a world of cinematic experiences and limitless possibilities.

This design marvel pushes boundaries with cutting-edge AI technology seamlessly integrated into a smoother, more sophisticated look. Notable design improvements, including a flat-screen display with a subtle curvature, stronger titanium construction, and thinner, more consistent bezels, redefine the aesthetic experience. The Galaxy S24 stands as a beacon of technological brilliance, combining style, functionality, and intelligence to elevate your smartphone experience to unprecedented heights. In a world where innovation knows no bounds, the future is now, and it rests in the palm of your hand.

CHAPTER ONE

SAMSUNG GALAXY SERIES EVOLUTION

The Samsung Galaxy series, born in the vibrant tapestry of the smartphone industry, has not merely thrived; it has shaped the very contours of technological progress. This comprehensive exploration embarks on a riveting journey, tracing the evolutionary footsteps of the Samsung Galaxy from its inception to its current pinnacle. A chronicle of innovation, design brilliance, and user-centric advancements unfolds, unraveling the dynamic narrative that defines the essence of the Galaxy series.

- **The Birth of a Pioneer**

In the annals of smartphone history, the Galaxy series emerged as a phoenix in 2010 with the launch of the Samsung Galaxy S. This chapter unfolds the foundational moments, delving into the strategic vision and technological prowess that marked the inception of the Galaxy series, laying the groundwork for what would become a transformative force.

- **Galaxy S and Note Series**

As the Galaxy series gained momentum, the introduction of flagship lines such as the Galaxy S and Note became keystones. This chapter meticulously traces the evolution of these series, unpacking the iterative advancements, defining features, and the symbiotic relationship that has characterized Samsung's commitment to excellence.

- **Design Philosophy and Materials**

An exploration of the Galaxy series is incomplete without scrutinizing its design evolution. From the utilitarian to the sublime, this chapter chronicles the metamorphosis of design philosophy, emphasizing the transition from plastic bodies to the embrace of premium materials, culminating in the iconic design language that epitomizes the Galaxy series.

- **Display Technologies**

The Galaxy series has long been synonymous with cutting-edge display technologies. This chapter unravels the saga of display evolution, from the adoption of vibrant AMOLED screens to the introduction of Infinity Displays, curved edges, HDR support, and high refresh rates, transforming the act of viewing into an immersive odyssey.

- **Camera Innovations**

At the core of the Galaxy series' allure lies its groundbreaking camera technology. This chapter takes a deep dive into the lens, exploring the journey from single-lens setups to the intricacies of multi-lens configurations, megapixel breakthroughs, and the integration of artificial intelligence, birthing a photographic symphony that captivates the senses.

- **Processing Prowess - Powering the Galaxy**

The heartbeat of the Galaxy lies in its processing power. From the early days of Exynos processors to collaborations with Qualcomm Snapdragon, this chapter scrutinizes the relentless pursuit of faster speeds, superior performance, and the infusion of artificial intelligence and machine learning, transforming smartphones into intelligent companions.

- **Connectivity Revolution - Network Evolution**

The Galaxy series has been at the forefront of connectivity revolutions. This chapter explores the transition from 4G to the groundbreaking integration of 5G technology, unveiling faster speeds, seamless connectivity, and the advent of wireless charging. Features like Reverse Wireless Power Share showcase Samsung's commitment to staying ahead in the connectivity race.

- **User-Centric Elegance - Software Experience**

The journey of the Galaxy series extends beyond hardware to a software experience that marries functionality with elegance. This chapter traverses the interface landscape, from the early days of TouchWiz to the present-day sophistication of One UI. It spotlights features like Samsung DeX and the robust security blanket of Samsung Knox, epitomizing user-centric design.

- **A Trailblazing Legacy**

As we conclude this odyssey through the Evolution of Samsung Galaxy, it's clear that the series is not just a collection of devices but a testament to Samsung's commitment to pioneering innovation. Each iteration has been a stepping stone, not just in the evolution of smartphones but in the shaping of our digital future. The legacy continues, and the Galaxy series remains a beacon, beckoning us towards the frontiers of what technology can achieve. The Evolution of Samsung Galaxy is a testament to the journey, the innovation, and the unwavering pursuit of excellence that defines this iconic series.

 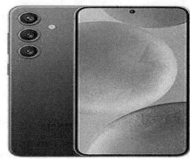

Unwrapping Samsung Galaxy S24

In the ever-evolving landscape of smartphones, Samsung once again takes center stage with the highly anticipated release of the Samsung Galaxy S24. This technological masterpiece represents the culmination of years of innovation, design prowess, and user-centric engineering. As we embark on the journey of unwrapping the Galaxy S24, we delve into the intricacies that make this device a beacon of excellence in the realm of mobile technology.

- **A Glimpse into the Future**

The Galaxy S24 is more than a mere device; it is a statement of the future. Delving into the grand unveiling, exploring the anticipation leading up to the launch event and the initial impressions that set the stage for what promises to be a groundbreaking addition to the Samsung Galaxy series.

- **Beyond Aesthetics**

Unwrapping the Galaxy S24 reveals a device that transcends mere aesthetics. Exploring the meticulous craftsmanship, premium materials, and ergonomic considerations that have shaped the physical allure of the S24. From color choices to form factor innovations, every detail contributes to an unrivaled sense of elegance.

- **The Infinity-O Dynamic AMOLED Display - Visual Immersion Redefined**

At the heart of the Galaxy S24's allure lies its display technology. This explores the brilliance of the Infinity-O Dynamic AMOLED display, unraveling the magic of vibrant colors, deep contrasts, and the introduction of a mesmerizing 120Hz ProMotion refresh rate. It's not just a screen; it's a portal to a visually immersive experience.

- **Quad Ultra Vision Camera System - Capturing Every Detail**

The camera technology of the Galaxy S24 takes center stage. From the remarkable 108MP main sensor to the intricacies of the Quad Ultra Vision Camera system, we unwrap the capabilities that redefine smartphone photography. Artificial intelligence enhancements and Night Vision technology paint a vivid picture of a device that captures every nuance.

- **Performance Beyond Limits - Exynos 7nm+ Octa-Core Processor**

The Galaxy S24 isn't just about aesthetics and imagery; it's a powerhouse beneath the surface. It peels back the layers of the Exynos 7nm+ Octa-Core processor, showcasing the raw performance, gaming capabilities, and efficiency that set new benchmarks in the smartphone industry.

- **5G Connectivity Redefined - A Glimpse into the Future of Connectivity**

In the era of 5G, the Galaxy S24 stands at the forefront of connectivity. It explores the seamless integration of 5G technology, reshaping the way we experience streaming, gaming, and communication. It's not just about speed; it's about staying ahead in the digital age.

- **Revamped Battery Technology - Powering Your Day**

Unwrapping the Galaxy S24 reveals not just performance but intelligent power management. It explores the adaptive power-saving mode, learning user behavior to optimize battery consumption. Bid farewell to battery anxiety as the S24 ensures longevity and efficient charging.

- **Immersive Entertainment Hub - Dolby Atmos Audio and More**

Beyond its primary functions, the Galaxy S24 transforms into an entertainment hub. This unwraps the Dolby Atmos audio technology, expanded storage capacity, and features that elevate your smartphone into a cinematic experience. It's not just a device; it's a gateway to a world of entertainment possibilities.

As we conclude the unwrapping journey of the Samsung Galaxy S24, it becomes apparent that this device isn't just a smartphone; it's a glimpse into the future of mobile technology. With its unparalleled design, cutting-edge display, powerful performance, and a myriad of features that cater to every aspect of a user's digital life, the Galaxy S24 stands as a testament to Samsung's commitment to innovation. The unwrapped Galaxy S24 isn't just a device in your hands; it's the future unfolding.

Significance of the Galaxy S24 in the Smartphone Landscape

The Samsung Galaxy S24's emphasis on cutting-edge AI technologies, which are intended to give consumers a more personalized and intuitive experience, is among its most noteworthy characteristics. Through the integration of cutting-edge artificial intelligence technology, Samsung hopes to revolutionize user interaction with smartphones and highlight the full potential of AI in mobile devices. The heart of Samsung's in-house AI helper and model, Gauss, is the Galaxy S24. The sophisticated AI capabilities of the Galaxy S24 are primarily powered by Gauss, which provides consumers with a plethora of features and advantages. Improved speech recognition, natural language comprehension, and real-time translation are just a few of the possible benefits and capabilities of Gauss, all of which add to a more smooth and effective user experience. Proactive outcomes for intricate tasks are also included in the AI features of the Galaxy S24. The smartphone can offer customized recommendations and suggestions based on usage patterns and commonly used apps, which are catered to the individual's requirements and inclinations. The Galaxy S24 can anticipate user needs and provide pertinent support thanks to this level of understanding, which simplifies daily tasks and increases productivity. Travel and destination analysis is yet another cutting-edge AI feature in the Galaxy S24. Users can be informed and ready for their travels with the help of the smartphone's real-time weather and traffic information capabilities. Moreover, the AI capabilities of the Galaxy S24 enable smooth integration with other app features, resulting in a unified and user-friendly experience.

> ### Technological Marvel - Setting the Bar Higher

At the heart of the Galaxy S24's significance lies its technological marvel. Meticulously dissects the groundbreaking features that make the S24 stand out, from the powerhouse Exynos 7nm+ Octa-Core processor to the Infinity-O Dynamic AMOLED display with its 120Hz ProMotion refresh rate. It is not merely a smartphone; it's a technological juggernaut that raises the bar for the entire industry.

> ### Design Excellence - Form Meets Functionality

The Galaxy S24 is not just a tool; it's a masterpiece of design excellence. Delving into the aesthetic significance of the S24, exploring the meticulous craftsmanship, premium materials, and ergonomic considerations that result in a device that is not only visually stunning but also a joy to hold and use. It exemplifies how form and functionality can coalesce to create a seamless user experience.

> ### Visual Brilliance - Infinity-O Dynamic AMOLED Display

The significance of the Galaxy S24 extends to its visual brilliance, epitomized by the Infinity-O Dynamic AMOLED display. This section unpacks the immersive experience offered by vibrant colors, deep blacks, and the smooth responsiveness of the 120Hz ProMotion refresh rate. The display isn't just a feature; it's a visual revolution that transforms how users interact with their smartphones.

➤ Photographic Mastery - Quad Ultra Vision Camera System

In an era where visual storytelling reigns supreme, the Galaxy S24's camera system takes center stage. It explores the significance of the Quad Ultra Vision Camera system, detailing the prowess of the 108MP main sensor, AI-driven enhancements, and NightVision technology. The S24 isn't just capturing moments; it's rewriting the standards for smartphone photography.

➤ Unmatched Performance - Exynos 7nm+ Octa-Core Processor

Performance is the heartbeat of the Galaxy S24, and scrutinizes the significance of the Exynos 7nm+ Octa-Core processor. From multitasking capabilities to gaming performance, the S24 showcases unmatched power and efficiency, setting a new benchmark for what users can expect from a smartphone.

➤ Connectivity Revolution - 5G Integration

The Galaxy S24 isn't just connected; it's a harbinger of the future of connectivity. It explores the significance of its seamless integration of 5G technology, ushering in faster data speeds, low latency, and transformative possibilities for streaming, gaming, and communication. It's not just about being connected; it's about staying ahead in the digital age.

➤ Adaptive Power Management - Intelligent Battery Technology

As smartphones become integral to daily life, battery management becomes paramount. It unravels the significance of the S24's adaptive power-saving mode, showcasing intelligent battery technology that adapts to individual usage patterns, ensuring longevity and adaptability. It's not just about lasting through the day; it's about a device that understands and aligns with your lifestyle.

➢ Robust Security Measures - Biometric Authentication

In an era where privacy is a priority, the Galaxy S24 introduces robust security measures. It explores the significance of advanced biometric authentication, combining facial recognition technology and an ultrasonic fingerprint sensor. The S24 isn't just a device; it's a fortress of security, ensuring user data remains private and protected.

The Samsung Galaxy S24 isn't just a smartphone; it's a pivotal force shaping the future of smartphones. Its significance extends beyond its individual features to the holistic user experience it provides. As the S24 takes its place in the smartphone landscape, it marks a turning point, redefining expectations and solidifying Samsung's position as an industry leader. It is not merely a device; it's a statement, a testament to innovation, and a symbol of what the future holds in the dynamic and ever-evolving world of smartphones.

CHAPTER TWO

DESIGN AND BUILD

Samsung is redesigning the Galaxy S24's design from the ground up. The 6.17-inch flat panel on the front remains comparable to its predecessor, but there are some noticeable changes to the side frames that give the device a somewhat different feel when held in the hand. As a change from earlier versions with rounded sides, the Galaxy S24 has a flat frame design. This design decision can make the device feel more squared away in the palm and elicit different feedback from consumers. The addition of a UWB (Ultra-Wideband) antenna on the side is one of the most noticeable design modifications. As part of their Galaxy phone lineup, Samsung is dedicating valuable real estate to UWB technology, which is a big first. There is a noticeable reduction in the bezels surrounding the screen. It looks from the video that one of the color options for the Galaxy S24 will be light blue. The anticipated dimensions of the upcoming Galaxy S24 are estimated to measure roughly 147 x 70.5 x 7.6 mm, making it slightly higher and less wide. The phone's waistline doesn't change in spite of these modifications.

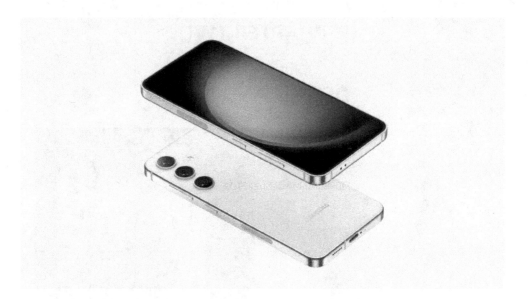

The phone's back panel is identical to that of its predecessor, with three cameras that each protrude separately from the frame and an LED flash. According to the renderings, the back panel will have a smooth matte finish that improves the tactile experience in the palm.

The design philosophy of the Galaxy S24 goes beyond mere aesthetics; it embodies a narrative. This dissects the core tenets of Samsung's design philosophy, exploring the balance between sleek modernity and timeless elegance. From the seamless integration of glass and metal to the thoughtful placement of physical buttons, every detail is a conscious choice in creating an aesthetic marvel.

➢ Ergonomic Considerations - Form Meets Comfort

The Galaxy S24 isn't just about looking good; it's designed for comfort and usability. This section explores the ergonomic considerations that make the S24 a joy to hold and operate. From the curvature of the edges to the placement of the fingerprint sensor, the design prioritizes user comfort without compromising on style. The choice of materials elevates the Galaxy S24 from a device to a work of art. It delves into the premium materials employed, from the robust metal frame to the Gorilla Glass protection on the front and back. The fusion of materials isn't just about durability; it's about creating a tactile and visually pleasing device that stands the test of time.

➢ A Symphony of Colors - Personalized Expression

The Galaxy S24 offers more than just a device; it's an extension of personal style. This section explores the diverse color palette choices available, each inspired by various elements, allowing users to express themselves through their device. The significance of color isn't merely cosmetic; it's about creating a personalized connection with the user. In the pursuit of design excellence, the Galaxy S24 introduces innovative form factors. This chapter explores design elements such as the bezel-less Infinity-O Dynamic AMOLED display and the subtle curvature of the edges, creating a visual experience that extends beyond the confines of conventional designs. It's not just a phone; it's a canvas for innovation.

➢ Durability and Resistance - Withstanding the Tests of Time

The design and build of the Galaxy S24 aren't just about aesthetics; they're about durability. This section delves into the engineering that makes the S24 resistant to the tests of time – from resisting scratches on the display to offering water and dust resistance. The S24 isn't just a delicate device; it's built to withstand the rigors of daily life. Symmetry is more than a visual choice; it's a design principle that creates harmony. This chapter explores how the Galaxy S24 achieves a sense of balance and symmetry, from the arrangement of camera modules to the placement of ports. It's not just about visual appeal; it's about creating a sense of unity in design.

it's about functionality and accessibility. This section explores features like the positioning of physical buttons, the intuitive interface of the One UI, and the strategic placement of the fingerprint sensor for seamless user interaction. The design isn't just for show; it's a tool for enhanced user experience. The design and build of the Samsung Galaxy S24 transcend the boundaries of conventional smartphones. It's not just a device; it's a harmonious blend of aesthetics, functionality, and durability. From the premium materials to the ergonomic considerations, every facet of the S24's design is a testament to Samsung's commitment to excellence. As users unwrap the Galaxy S24, they don't just hold a phone; they hold a piece of design and engineering brilliance in the palm of their hands.

Aesthetic Marvel: The Ergonomic Design

The Samsung Galaxy S24 is not just a technological marvel but a true aesthetic delight, and at the forefront of its visual allure is the meticulously crafted ergonomic design. Every curve, every line, and every detail has been purposefully considered, resulting in a device that seamlessly blends form and function.

1. **Sleek Symmetry:** The Galaxy S24 boasts a sleek and symmetrical design that exudes a sense of harmony. The front and back panels converge effortlessly into the aluminum frame, creating a device that feels as good in the hand as it looks.

2. **Infinity Display:** The device is adorned with an expansive Infinity Display that stretches from edge to edge, providing an immersive visual experience. The bezels are artfully minimized, allowing the screen to take center stage and drawing you into a world of vibrant colors and sharp contrasts.

3. **Premium Materials:** Crafted with premium materials, the Samsung Galaxy S24 feels like a luxurious accessory. Whether it's the smooth glass back, the robust aluminum frame, or the precisely engineered buttons, each element contributes to a feeling of sophistication and durability.

4. **Intuitive Button Placement:** The placement of buttons and controls is intuitive, ensuring easy accessibility without compromising the aesthetic appeal. Every button press is a tactile pleasure, adding to the overall user experience.

5. **Distinctive Camera Module:** The camera module is not just a functional component but a distinctive design element. Its placement and arrangement are thoughtfully integrated into the overall design, contributing to a visual identity that is uniquely Samsung.

6. **Slim Profile:** Despite its powerful capabilities, the Galaxy S24 maintains a remarkably slim profile. The engineers have succeeded in packing cutting-edge technology into a device that not only performs at the highest level but also feels remarkably lightweight and portable.

7. **Color Palette Choices:** The aesthetic charm extends to the range of color options available. From timeless classics to bold and vibrant hues, the color palette choices allow users to express their personal style while enjoying a device that is undeniably elegant.

8. **Attention to Detail:** It's the small details that truly elevate the design of the Samsung Galaxy S24. From the precisely chamfered edges to the way the light dances on the surface, every detail has

been considered, reinforcing the commitment to creating a device that is as much a visual masterpiece as it is a technological powerhouse.

In essence, the Samsung Galaxy S24 transcends mere functionality to become a true aesthetic marvel. It is a testament to Samsung's dedication to not only meet the technological demands of users but also to delight the senses with a design that is as beautiful as it is functional.

Premium Build Materials

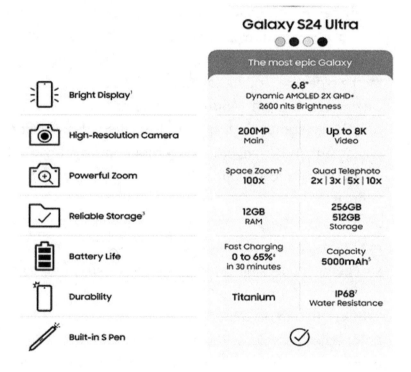

	Galaxy S24 Ultra	
	The most epic Galaxy	
Bright Display[1]	6.8" Dynamic AMOLED 2X QHD+ 2600 nits Brightness	
High-Resolution Camera	200MP Main	Up to 8K Video
Powerful Zoom	Space Zoom[2] 100x	Quad Telephoto 2x | 3x | 5x | 10x
Reliable Storage[3]	12GB RAM	256GB 512GB Storage
Battery Life	Fast Charging 0 to 65%[4] in 30 minutes	Capacity 5000mAh[5]
Durability	Titanium	IP68[7] Water Resistance
Built-in S Pen	⊘	

Galaxy S24

Everyday epic

6.2"
Dynamic AMOLED 2X FHD+
2600 nits Brightness

50MP Main	Up to 8K Video
Space Zoom² 30x	Dual Telephoto 2x | 3x
8GB RAM	128GB 256GB Storage
Fast Charging 0 to 50%⁶ in 30 minutes	Capacity 4000mAh⁵
Armor Aluminum 2.0	IP68⁷ Water Resistance

Standard features

 Snapdragon® 8 Gen 3 Processor   Dynamic Lock Screen   Smart Keyboard  Security and Privacy Protected by Knox

The Samsung Galaxy S24 is a pinnacle of craftsmanship, embodying a commitment to excellence with its premium build materials. Every detail of its construction reflects a dedication to quality, durability, and an unmistakable sense of luxury. **Here's a closer look at the premium build materials that define the Samsung Galaxy S24:**

- **Glass Unibody:** The Galaxy S24 boasts a seamless glass unibody construction, creating a device that feels incredibly smooth and premium to the touch. The front and back panels seamlessly blend into the sturdy aluminum frame, providing both durability and a sleek aesthetic.
- **Corning Gorilla Glass Victus**: The device features the latest Corning Gorilla Glass Victus on both the front and back. This

advanced glass technology not only enhances scratch resistance but also provides exceptional drop protection, ensuring that the Galaxy S24 maintains its pristine appearance even in the face of daily wear and tear.

- **Aluminum Frame:** The robust aluminum frame not only contributes to the device's structural integrity but also adds a touch of sophistication. The precisely crafted frame seamlessly integrates with the glass panels, creating a cohesive and durable structure.

- **Metallic Accents:** Delicate metallic accents further elevate the Galaxy S24's premium aesthetic. From the refined buttons to the precisely crafted camera module, these metallic details add a sense of luxury and attention to detail.

- **Water and Dust Resistance:** The Galaxy S24 is designed to withstand the elements with an IP68 rating for water and dust resistance. This engineering feat ensures that the device remains resilient, providing peace of mind for users in various environments.

- **Thin Form Factor:** Despite its robust build, the Galaxy S24 maintains a remarkably thin form factor. This achievement not only contributes to the device's overall elegance but also enhances the user's comfort and convenience.

- **Weight Distribution:** The careful consideration of weight distribution makes the Galaxy S24 comfortable to hold and use. The strategic placement of premium materials ensures that the device feels balanced, avoiding any unnecessary strain during prolonged usage.

- **Premium Finishes:** The Samsung Galaxy S24 is available in a range of premium finishes, from classic to contemporary. Each finish is meticulously applied, adding depth and character to the device and allowing users to choose a style that resonates with their personal preferences.

The Samsung Galaxy S24's premium build materials represent a harmonious fusion of form and function. From its glass unibody to the metallic accents, every component is a testament to Samsung's unwavering commitment to delivering a device that not only performs at the highest level but also stands as a symbol of refined elegance.

Color Palette Selections and Their Inspirations

In the creation of the Samsung Galaxy S24, every detail has been meticulously curated, and the color palette is no exception. The color selections for this flagship device transcend the ordinary, offering users not just a phone but a canvas of self-expression. Delving into the inspirations behind the color palette selections of the Samsung Galaxy S24 and the emotions they evoke.

A. Mystic Black:
- **Inspiration:** Elegance and Sophistication

Mystic Black embodies timeless sophistication. Inspired by the deep, mysterious allure of the night, this color choice reflects the epitome of class and luxury. The sleek, jet-black hue not only exudes refinement but also serves as a blank canvas for the vibrant screen to take center stage.

B. Prism White:
- **Inspiration:** Purity and Luminescence

Prism White draws inspiration from the enchanting play of light. Like a prism reflecting a spectrum of colors, these variant captures purity and luminescence. The immaculate white surface is a canvas for refracted light, creating a captivating visual display that mirrors the vibrancy of the world around us.

C. Aurora Blue:
- **Inspiration:** Nature's Spectacle

Aurora Blue is a homage to the breathtaking natural phenomena found in the Earth's polar regions. Just like the dancing lights of the aurora borealis, this color palette evokes a sense of wonder and awe. The subtle gradient captures the essence of a constantly shifting, dynamic landscape.

D. Sunset Gold:
- **Inspiration:** Warmth and Radiance

Sunset Gold takes cues from the glorious hues of a setting sun. The warm and radiant tones embody a sense of comfort and tranquility. With every glance, users are reminded of the beauty of a sunset, creating a harmonious connection between the device and the serenity of nature.

E. Coral Pink:
- **Inspiration:** Playful Energy

Coral Pink bursts with playful energy and vibrancy. Drawing inspiration from the coral reefs teeming with life and color, this variant captures the spirit of joy and spontaneity. It serves as a bold statement for those who seek to infuse their lives with a touch of exuberance.

F. Quantum Silver:
- **Inspiration:** Technological Futurism

Quantum Silver is a testament to technological futurism. Mirroring the sleek and polished surfaces of advanced machinery, this color palette represents the cutting edge of innovation. It is a modern and sophisticated choice for those who embrace the future with confidence.

G. Earth Green:
- **Inspiration:** Nature's Bounty

Earth Green finds its roots in the lush landscapes of nature. Inspired by the rich, calming greens of the Earth, this variant is a nod to environmental consciousness. It serves as a reminder of the beauty that surrounds us and the importance of preserving our planet.

The color palette selections for the Samsung Galaxy S24 are more than just aesthetic choices; they are carefully crafted expressions of inspiration and emotion. From the timeless Mystic Black to the playful Coral Pink, each variant offers users a unique journey through color, allowing them to choose a device that not only suits their lifestyle but resonates with their individual spirit. The Galaxy S24 is not just a smartphone; it is a work of art, and its color palette is the brushstroke that brings it to life.

Crafting a Sleek and Durable Device

In the relentless pursuit of technological excellence, Samsung has once again set a new standard with the Galaxy S24, a device that seamlessly marries sleek aesthetics with unwavering durability. From the drawing board to the hands of the user, every step in crafting this device reflects a commitment to delivering an unparalleled user experience.

- ➤ **Innovative Materials:** The foundation of the Galaxy S24's design lies in the careful selection of materials. The device features a sleek glass unibody that not only exudes a premium feel but also contributes to a seamless and refined aesthetic. The use of Corning Gorilla Glass Victus ensures superior protection against scratches and drops, reinforcing the device's durability without compromising on elegance.

- ➤ **Structural Integrity:** Crafted with precision, the Galaxy S24 boasts a robust aluminum frame that not only adds structural integrity but also provides a premium feel when held. The meticulous engineering of the frame contributes to the device's slim profile, creating a harmonious balance between form and function.

- ➤ **Water and Dust Resistance:** The Galaxy S24 is designed to accompany users on all life's adventures. With an IP68 rating for water and dust resistance, the device offers peace of mind in various environments. Whether facing unexpected rain or accidental spills, the Galaxy S24 stands ready to weather the elements.

- ➤ **Rigorous Testing:** Samsung's commitment to durability extends beyond theoretical design to real-world testing. The Galaxy S24 undergoes rigorous testing processes to ensure it can withstand the demands of daily use. From drop tests to temperature and humidity trials, every aspect is scrutinized to guarantee reliability and longevity.

- ➤ **Slim Form Factor:** Despite its robust build, the Galaxy S24 maintains a remarkably slim form factor. The engineering team at Samsung has skillfully balanced durability with aesthetics, creating a device that not only fits comfortably in the hand but also slips effortlessly into pockets and purses.

- ➤ **Corrosion-Resistant Components:** Recognizing the importance of long-term reliability, the Galaxy S24 incorporates corrosion-resistant components. This feature not only extends the device's lifespan but also ensures that it retains its polished appearance over time, standing the test of continuous usage.

➢ **Attention to Detail:** The devil is in the details, and Samsung leaves no stone unturned. Every button, every connection point, and every seam are meticulously crafted to ensure a flawless user experience. The attention to detail not only enhances the device's aesthetic appeal but also contributes to its overall durability.

➢ **Sustainable Design:** In a nod to environmental responsibility, the Galaxy S24 is crafted with sustainability in mind. Samsung embraces eco-friendly practices in the manufacturing process, choosing materials and methods that minimize environmental impact without compromising the device's quality or performance.

The Samsung Galaxy S24 is a testament to the art of crafting a device that transcends the ordinary. It embodies the perfect symbiosis of sleek aesthetics and robust durability, offering users not just a smartphone but a companion that can withstand the rigors of modern life while exuding timeless elegance. The Galaxy S24 is more than a device; it is a masterpiece born from the fusion of cutting-edge technology and refined craftsmanship.

CHAPTER THREE

DISPLAY TECHNOLOGY

Display technology is a dynamic field, continually evolving to deliver better visual experiences, improved energy efficiency, and innovative form factors across a wide range of electronic devices. Display technology refers to the methods and technologies used to showcase visual information on electronic devices, such as smartphones, televisions, computer monitors, and more. It encompasses a range of technologies and techniques aimed at presenting images, videos, and graphics in a clear, vibrant, and engaging manner. the display technology in the Samsung Galaxy S24 isn't just a feature; it's a revelation. Join us as we explore the immersive visual journey that awaits—a journey where every glance at the Galaxy S24's display is an invitation to witness the future of smartphone innovation.

10MP
3x Optical Zoom

50MP
Wide-angle & 2x Optical Quality Zoom

12MP
Ultra Wide[11]

12MP
Selfie Camera

SAMSUNG GALAXY S24

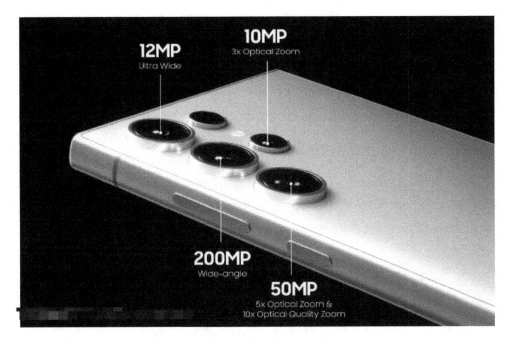

SAMSUNG GALAXY S24 ULTRA

Infinity-O Dynamic AMOLED Display

The Samsung Galaxy S24 boasts an immersive Infinity-O Dynamic AMOLED display, a technological marvel that redefines the visual experience on smartphones. Elevating the Samsung Galaxy S24 to extraordinary heights is its magnificent Infinity-O Dynamic AMOLED display—a true technological masterpiece that transcends the conventional smartphone visual experience. This immersive display represents a paradigm shift, setting new standards for brilliance, precision, and engagement. Allow me to introduce you to the captivating realm of the Galaxy S24's display, where every glance becomes a journey into the future of smartphone innovation.

Infinity-O Design

The Infinity-O display on the Galaxy S24 introduces a captivating design with minimal bezels, pushing the boundaries of screen real estate. The "O" in Infinity-O signifies a precisely placed camera cutout, ensuring a seamless and immersive viewing experience without sacrificing essential front-facing camera functionality.

Dynamic AMOLED Brilliance

Powered by Dynamic AMOLED technology, the Galaxy S24's display delivers unparalleled vibrancy, contrast, and clarity. Each pixel is individually lit, producing deep blacks, vibrant colors, and an infinite contrast ratio. This technology ensures that every image, video, and graphical element is presented with stunning precision.

The Galaxy S24's display is equipped with an adaptive refresh rate, intelligently adjusting to the content being viewed. Whether you're scrolling through text, watching videos, or engaging in high-speed gaming, the refresh rate dynamically optimizes for a seamless and energy-efficient performance, providing smooth transitions and an ultra-responsive touch experience. With HDR10+ certification, the Galaxy S24 delivers a pro-grade HDR viewing experience. High Dynamic Range enhances the display's ability to showcase a broader range of colors and contrasts, allowing users to enjoy content with exceptional detail, whether they're streaming the latest movies or capturing HDR-enhanced photos. The Galaxy S24's display boasts a WQHD+ resolution, ensuring that every detail is presented with sharpness and clarity. Whether you're viewing documents, images, or multimedia content, the precision of the display contributes to a visually stunning and immersive experience. This display technology transforms multimedia interaction into an immersive journey. From watching videos to gaming and exploring augmented reality applications, the Galaxy S24's Infinity-O Dynamic AMOLED display actively engages users, delivering a captivating and visually enriching experience. Seamlessly integrated beneath the display is the Ultrasonic Under-Display Fingerprint Sensor. This advanced biometric security feature not only adds an extra layer of protection but also maintains the sleek aesthetic of the Infinity-O display, allowing users to unlock their device with a simple touch on the screen.

In conclusion, the combination of the Infinity-O design and Dynamic AMOLED technology in the Samsung Galaxy S24 results in a display that is not just a window to the digital world but a portal to a visually stunning and immersive experience. The Galaxy S24's display technology embodies Samsung's commitment to pushing the boundaries of what's possible, offering users a display that is both a work of art and a functional masterpiece.

ProMotion Refresh Rate: A Visual Feast

Introducing the Samsung Galaxy S24, a device that sets a new standard for visual excellence with its ProMotion Refresh Rate feature. This cutting-edge technology transforms your smartphone experience into a visual feast, offering unprecedented smoothness and responsiveness.

➢ **ProMotion Brilliance:** At the heart of the Galaxy S24 lies the ProMotion Refresh Rate, a feature that redefines how you perceive visuals on your smartphone. Witness a level of brilliance and fluidity that goes beyond the ordinary, elevating the display's responsiveness to an unparalleled standard.

➢ **Adaptive Refresh Rate Mastery:** The ProMotion Refresh Rate isn't just about high numbers; it's about adaptability. The display dynamically adjusts its refresh rate based on the content you're engaging with. Whether you're scrolling through text, playing games, or watching videos, the Galaxy S24 optimizes the refresh rate in real-time for a seamlessly smooth experience.

- ➤ **Smooth Transitions, Seamless Interactions:** Experience transitions like never before—smooth, fluid, and virtually instantaneous. The ProMotion Refresh Rate ensures that every interaction, from swiping through apps to navigating menus, is a delightfully seamless experience, responding to your touch with a level of precision that redefines user interaction.
- ➤ **Optimized Energy Efficiency:** While delivering a visual feast, the ProMotion Refresh Rate is also designed with energy efficiency in mind. It intelligently adjusts the refresh rate to match the demands of your activities, optimizing power consumption without compromising on the stunning visual experience.
- ➤ **Enhanced Gaming and Multimedia:** For gamers and multimedia enthusiasts, the ProMotion Refresh Rate takes your experience to the next level. Enjoy gaming with ultra-smooth frame rates and a responsiveness that puts you in control. Immerse yourself in multimedia content with visuals that captivate and engage, making every moment on the Galaxy S24 a true cinematic adventure.
- ➤ **Precision in Motion:** Whether you're exploring high-resolution images, viewing detailed documents, or simply navigating your device, the ProMotion Refresh Rate ensures that motion is presented with precision. Enjoy a level of clarity and detail that enhances the overall visual aesthetics of the Galaxy S24.

ProMotion Refresh Rate in the Samsung Galaxy S24 isn't just a feature; it's a visual spectacle. It's about bringing a level of fluidity and responsiveness that transforms your smartphone interactions into a truly captivating experience. Welcome to a world where every swipe, scroll, and touch on the Galaxy S24 is a testament to the brilliance of ProMotion technology.

Adaptive Brightness and HDR10+ Support

Immerse yourself in a visual spectacle with the Samsung Galaxy S24, where Adaptive Brightness and HDR10+ Support join forces to redefine, your smartphone viewing experience.

- **Adaptive Brilliance:**

The Galaxy S24 introduces Adaptive Brightness, a feature that dynamically adjusts your screen's brightness based on your surroundings. Seamlessly transitioning from bright daylight to ambient indoor lighting, this intelligent technology ensures optimal visibility while conserving energy, providing a viewing experience tailored to your environment.

- **HDR10+ Excellence:**

Prepare for a cinematic journey with HDR10+ Support. The Galaxy S24 brings you pro-grade High Dynamic Range (HDR) capabilities, enhancing every image and video with a broader spectrum of colors and richer contrasts. Whether you're streaming content or capturing memories, witness visuals that transcend ordinary smartphone displays.

- **Adapting to Ambient Light:**

Adaptive Brightness goes beyond manual adjustments. By analyzing ambient light levels, the Galaxy S24 intuitively fine-tunes its brightness, ensuring your display remains comfortably visible without straining your eyes. Say goodbye to squinting under the sun or fumbling in the dark—the Galaxy S24 adapts to your every environment.

- **Cinematic Visuals with HDR10+:**

HDR10+ Support transforms your Galaxy S24 into a portable cinema. Revel in content that comes alive with enhanced vibrancy and detail.

From captivating movies to your own HDR-enhanced photos, each visual moment is a masterpiece of color accuracy and dynamic range.

- **Optimized Power Efficiency:**

Adaptive Brightness isn't just about comfort; it's about efficiency. By automatically adjusting brightness levels, the Galaxy S24 optimizes power consumption. Enjoy prolonged battery life without compromising on the stunning visual experience—a perfect balance between brilliance and energy conservation.

- **Enhanced Multimedia Enjoyment:**

With HDR10+ Support, your multimedia experience reaches new heights. Immerse yourself in games, videos, and photos that pop with lifelike colors and depth. The Galaxy S24 ensures that every visual encounter is a feast for the eyes, capturing the nuances that elevate your content consumption.

- **Seamless Day-to-Night Transition:**

Bid farewell to abrupt changes in brightness. Adaptive Brightness smoothly transitions your display from day to night, maintaining an optimal balance between visibility and eye comfort. Your Galaxy S24 adapts seamlessly to your surroundings, ensuring a visual experience that's gentle on the eyes.

The Adaptive Brightness and HDR10+ Support in the Samsung Galaxy S24 redefine what you can expect from a smartphone display. It's not just about adaptive intelligence; it's about creating a visual narrative that adapts to your environment and content, ensuring that every glance at your Galaxy S24 is a breathtaking encounter with brilliance. Welcome to a world where your smartphone display is as dynamic as your lifestyle. Explore the cutting-edge display capabilities of the

Samsung Galaxy 2024, where Adaptive Brightness and HDR10+ Support join forces to redefine your visual experience.

Crafting the Perfect Viewing Experience

Welcome to a realm where viewing becomes an art form—the Samsung Galaxy S24 is not just a smartphone; it's a canvas meticulously designed

- **Infinity-O Dynamic AMOLED Display:**

Embark on a visual odyssey with the Galaxy S24's Infinity-O Dynamic AMOLED display. The bezel-minimized design seamlessly extends from edge to edge, immersing you in a captivating world of vibrant colors and unprecedented clarity. The strategically placed camera cutout adds to the immersive canvas, ensuring an uninterrupted viewing experience.

- **ProMotion Refresh Rate:**

Experience the magic of fluidity with the ProMotion Refresh Rate. Every interaction on the Galaxy S24 is a visual delight, as the display adapts dynamically to your activities. From seamless transitions to ultra-responsive touch interactions, this feature ensures that your smartphone experience is as smooth as it is visually stunning.

- **Adaptive Brightness Intelligence:**

Step into a world of visual comfort with Adaptive Brightness. Your Galaxy S24 intuitively adjusts its brightness based on ambient lighting conditions, ensuring optimal visibility without compromising on power efficiency. Whether you're under the sun's glare or nestled in the dimness of your room, the display adapts to provide the perfect illumination.

- **HDR10+ Certification:**

The Galaxy S24 embraces cinema-grade visuals with HDR10+ certification. Every image and video come to life with enhanced color accuracy and dynamic contrasts. From streaming HDR-enhanced content to capturing photos, your viewing experience is elevated to pro-grade levels.

- **WQHD+ Precision:**

Witness every detail in stunning clarity with the WQHD+ resolution. Whether you're engrossed in documents, images, or multimedia content, the Galaxy S24's precision ensures that every pixel contributes to a visually enriching experience.

- **Ultrasonic Under-Display Fingerprint Sensor:**

Seamlessly integrated beneath the display, the Ultrasonic Under-Display Fingerprint Sensor adds a touch of sophistication to your viewing interaction. Unlock your device effortlessly, blending security with convenience without disrupting the immersive visual aesthetics.

- **Adaptive Refresh for Gaming Excitement:**

For gaming enthusiasts, the Adaptive Refresh Rate takes your gaming experience to the next level. Enjoy ultra-smooth frame rates, responsive controls, and a level of visual excitement that puts you in the heart of the action.

- **Eye Comfort Shield:**

Caring for your well-being, the Galaxy S24 introduces the Eye Comfort Shield. This feature automatically adjusts blue light emissions based on the time of day, reducing eye strain and promoting healthier viewing habits, especially during nighttime use.

In essence, the Samsung Galaxy S24 is a testament to the art of crafting the perfect viewing experience. Every feature, from the Infinity-O Dynamic AMOLED display to the ProMotion Refresh Rate and Adaptive Brightness Intelligence, is meticulously designed to ensure that your visual encounters are nothing short of extraordinary. Welcome to a new era of smartphone innovation where every glance at your Galaxy S24 is an invitation to indulge in the perfection of visual brilliance.

CHAPTER FOUR

CAMERA TECHNOLOGY

Embark on a revolutionary visual journey with the camera technology of the Samsung Galaxy S24—an extraordinary testament to innovation and precision in the realm of mobile photography. In the heart of the Samsung Galaxy S24 lies a sophisticated camera system designed to capture brilliance in every frame. This isn't just a camera; it's a gateway to a world where each photo is a visual story waiting to be told. The Galaxy S24 boasts a triple-lens configuration that redefines versatility. From wide-angle vistas to telephoto precision and macro marvels, the camera system adapts seamlessly to your creative vision, ensuring that every shot is a true reflection of your perspective. Elevating night photography to new heights, the Galaxy S24 introduces revolutionary low-light capabilities. Capture the essence of the night with clarity and detail, unlocking a realm of possibilities that extends far beyond the limitations of traditional smartphone cameras. Experience photography with an intuitive touch, thanks to AI-powered intelligence woven into the camera technology. From scene optimization to automatic adjustments, the Galaxy S24 ensures that every photo is a product of smart, adaptive photography that understands and enhances your subject matter.

The camera technology isn't confined to just photography—the Galaxy S24 raises the bar for video recording. Unleash your storytelling prowess with pro-grade video capabilities, allowing you to capture and share moments in cinematic clarity and precision. Witness the seamless integration of innovation with the under-display front camera. Minimizing interruptions to the expansive Infinity-O Dynamic AMOLED display, this discreet yet powerful front camera ensures that your selfies are as stunning as your rear-camera shots.

Unleash your creativity with an array of smart shooting modes. From intelligent scene recognition to fun-filled AR experiences, the Galaxy S24's camera technology invites you to explore and experiment, transforming ordinary moments into extraordinary memories. With the Galaxy S24, photography is reimagined as a dynamic and immersive experience. Each click is an opportunity to explore the boundaries of your creativity, supported by a camera system that empowers you to capture, share, and relive the moments that define your narrative.

In the world of the Samsung Galaxy S24, the camera isn't just a feature—it's a storyteller, an artist, and a companion on your visual adventures. Join us as we unravel the intricacies of camera technology that redefine the very essence of mobile photography, turning every capture into a masterpiece.

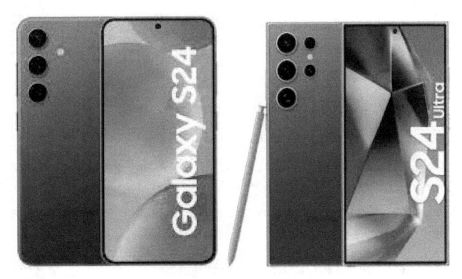

Quad Ultra Vision Camera System

Unveiling the Samsung Galaxy S24 and its Quad Ultra Vision Camera System—a pinnacle of mobile photography that transcends conventional boundaries, capturing moments with unprecedented clarity, precision, and artistic finesse. Let's embark on a comprehensive exploration of this revolutionary camera technology that redefines what's possible in smartphone photography.

- **The Essence of Quad Ultra Vision:**

At the core of the Galaxy S24's photographic prowess lies the Quad Ultra Vision Camera System—a sophisticated ensemble of four lenses meticulously crafted to deliver a transformative imaging experience. This isn't merely a camera; it's a visual storyteller equipped to capture the world in exquisite detail.

- **Versatile Lens Configuration:**

The Quad Ultra Vision Camera System encompasses a versatile quartet of lenses, each with a distinct purpose. From a high-resolution main lens for everyday captures to an ultra-wide-angle lens that expands your vistas, a telephoto lens for precise zooming, and a dedicated macro lens for close-up marvels, this system adapts to your every photographic need.

- **Revolutionary Low-Light Mastery:**

Bid farewell to limitations in low-light environments. The Galaxy S24's camera system introduces revolutionary low-light performance, capturing scenes in the nuances of night with remarkable clarity. The Quad Ultra Vision Camera System redefines nighttime photography, revealing details that were once shrouded in darkness.

- **AI-Powered Photography Intelligence:**

Elevating the art of photography, the Quad Ultra Vision Camera System incorporates AI-powered intelligence. Scene optimization, automatic adjustments, and intelligent recognition capabilities ensure that each shot is meticulously crafted to enhance the inherent beauty of your subject matter.

- **Pro-Grade Video Excellence:**

The camera system isn't confined to still photography—the Galaxy S24 pushes the boundaries of video recording with pro-grade capabilities. Cinematic clarity, dynamic range, and fluid motion capture empower you to tell your stories with a level of detail and precision that rivals professional videography.

- **Under-Display Front Camera Integration:**

Seamlessly integrated beneath the expansive Infinity-O Dynamic AMOLED display is the under-display front camera. This discreet yet powerful addition minimizes interruptions, ensuring that your selfies are as captivating as your rear-camera captures, contributing to the device's sleek and immersive design.

- **Smart Shooting Modes for Creativity:**

Unlock your creative potential with a plethora of smart shooting modes. Whether it's AI-driven scene recognition, playful AR experiences, or specialized modes for unique photographic scenarios, the Quad Ultra Vision Camera System transforms every photo opportunity into an exploration of creativity.

- **Photography Redefined:**

With the Galaxy S24, photography is redefined as an immersive and dynamic experience. The Quad Ultra Vision Camera System empowers you to capture the essence of every moment, from expansive landscapes to intricate details, with a level of sophistication that mirrors your artistic vision.

In essence, the Quad Ultra Vision Camera System in the Samsung Galaxy S24 isn't just a technological feature—it's a revolution in mobile photography. It's a gateway to a world where every click is a testament to the fusion of cutting-edge technology and artistic expression, turning every capture into a masterpiece of visual storytelling.

108MP Main Sensor: Unleashing the Power of Detail

Step into the realm of unprecedented detail with the Samsung Galaxy S24, featuring a groundbreaking 108MP Main Sensor that redefines the possibilities of smartphone photography. Let's explore how this high-resolution marvel unleashes a new era of imaging precision, capturing every nuance with unparalleled clarity. At the heart of the Galaxy S24's camera system is its extraordinary 108MP Main Sensor. This colossal sensor is not just a numerical feat; it's a technological powerhouse that allows you to capture images with an astonishing level of detail. With each shot, you're unleashing the power of 108 million pixels—a resolution previously reserved for professional-grade cameras. Witness a level of detail that goes beyond imagination. The 108MP Main Sensor captures scenes with such precision that every element, from distant landscapes to intricate textures, is rendered with unparalleled clarity. Whether you're zooming in on a single leaf or capturing a sweeping panorama, the Galaxy S24 transforms your photos into visual masterpieces.

- **Enhanced Zoom Capabilities:**

The high resolution of the 108MP Main Sensor isn't just about large file sizes—it's about unlocking enhanced zoom capabilities. Experience the freedom to zoom in on your subjects without compromising detail. The Galaxy S24 ensures that even when you zoom, the richness and clarity of your photos remain intact, delivering a zooming experience like never before.

- **Revolutionizing Low-Light Photography:**

Low-light environments are no challenge for the Galaxy S24's 108MP Main Sensor. Experience a revolution in low-light photography as the sensor's immense pixel size captures more light, resulting in brighter and clearer night shots. The era of capturing stunning details in the dark has arrived.

- **AI-Driven Scene Optimization:**

Intelligently harnessing the power of AI, the 108MP Main Sensor contributes to scene optimization. Whether you're capturing a vibrant cityscape or a serene sunset, the sensor, coupled with AI algorithms, ensures that each shot is finely tuned for optimal color balance, contrast, and overall brilliance.

- **Professional-Grade Photography:**

With the 108MP Main Sensor, the Galaxy S24 elevates your photography to professional-grade levels. Immerse yourself in the world of high-resolution imaging, where your smartphone becomes a tool for capturing moments with a level of clarity and detail that transcends ordinary photography.

- **Limitless Creativity:**

Unleash your creativity without limitations. The Galaxy S24's 108MP Main Sensor empowers you to explore new dimensions of photography, offering a canvas where every detail, every texture, and every shade is captured with such finesse that your creations become a true reflection of your artistic vision.

The108MP Main Sensor in the Samsung Galaxy S24 is not just a feature; it's a game-changer in the world of mobile photography. It's about pushing the boundaries of what's possible, capturing details that were once unimaginable, and turning every photo into a testament to the extraordinary capabilities of modern smartphone imaging technology.

AI-Driven Enhancements for Superlative Photography

Experience a new era of photographic excellence with the Samsung Galaxy S24, where AI-driven enhancements redefine the boundaries of smartphone photography. delving into the innovative technologies that harness the power of artificial intelligence, elevating your photo captures to a superlative level of brilliance.

- **Intelligent Scene Recognition:**

The Galaxy S24 introduces an advanced AI-driven system that elevates scene recognition to a whole new level. With the ability to analyze scenes in real-time, the device intelligently identifies various elements, from landscapes to portraits, adjusting settings to ensure each photo is optimized for the specific context. The result? Superlative photography tailored to the nuances of every moment.

- **Adaptive Exposure and Dynamic Range:**

Say goodbye to underexposed shadows and overblown highlights. The Galaxy S24's AI-driven enhancements intelligently adjust exposure levels and dynamic range, ensuring that your photos capture a balanced spectrum of light and shadow. Whether you're in challenging lighting conditions or capturing high-contrast scenes, each shot emerges with superlative clarity and detail.

- **Smart Composition Assistance:**

Empowering your creative vision, the Galaxy S24's AI-driven enhancements extend to composition assistance. The device intelligently analyzes the framing of your shots, offering real-time suggestions for optimal composition. From rule-of-thirds guidance to symmetry recommendations, you're equipped with AI assistance that transforms your photography into a superlative art form.

Enhanced Portrait Mode with AI Bokeh:

Elevate your portrait photography with AI-driven enhancements that redefine the art of bokeh. The Galaxy S24 intelligently identifies subjects in real-time, precisely applying background blur for a professional-looking bokeh effect. The result is superlative portrait shots where the subject takes center stage, framed by a seamlessly blurred background.

- **AI-Powered Night Mode Brilliance:**

Embrace the night with AI-powered Night Mode brilliance. The Galaxy S24's advanced algorithms analyze low-light scenarios, enhancing details and reducing noise to deliver superlative night-time captures. Every shot under the moonlit sky becomes a masterpiece, showcasing the power of AI-driven enhancements in low-light photography.

- **Automated Image Enhancement:**

Witness your photos undergo a transformative process with automated image enhancement. The Galaxy S24's AI-driven algorithms automatically identify areas that could benefit from enhancement, adjusting color tones, sharpness, and details to ensure each photo reaches its superlative potential. The result is a collection of images that consistently impress with their visual richness.

- **Superior Selfies with AI Beautification**

Elevate your selfie game with AI-driven beautification. The Galaxy S24's front camera utilizes AI algorithms to intelligently enhance facial features, providing a natural and flattering look. Say goodbye to manual editing—AI beautification ensures that your selfies are consistently superlative, effortlessly highlighting your best features.

- **Adaptive Focus and Object Tracking**

Capture moving subjects with unparalleled precision using AI-driven adaptive focus and object tracking. The Galaxy S24 intelligently tracks subjects in motion, adjusting focus dynamically to ensure superlative clarity. Whether it's a fast-paced sports event or a playful pet, every moment is captured with utmost detail.

AI-driven enhancements in the Samsung Galaxy S24 redefine the essence of superlative photography. With intelligent scene recognition, adaptive exposure, enhanced portrait capabilities, and more, the device becomes a creative ally, ensuring that each photo you capture is not just good but superlative—a testament to the synergy of artificial intelligence and cutting-edge smartphone photography.

NightVision Technology: Redefining Low-Light Photography

Embark on a nocturnal adventure with the Samsung Galaxy S24, where NightVision Technology redefines the boundaries of low-light photography. Explore how this groundbreaking feature enhances your nighttime captures, transforming moments in the dark into visually stunning masterpieces.

The Evolution of Night Photography:

The Galaxy S24 introduces NightVision Technology, a revolutionary leap in low-light photography. With advanced algorithms and cutting-edge sensor capabilities, this feature transcends traditional limitations, enabling you to capture the essence of the night with unprecedented clarity and detail.

- **Enhanced Sensitivity to Light:**

NightVision Technology is designed to significantly boost the device's sensitivity to light in low-lit environments. The Galaxy S24's sensor, coupled with intelligent algorithms, ensures that even the faintest sources of light are captured with enhanced brightness and clarity. Witness a new level of visibility in the dark that goes beyond the capabilities of standard smartphone cameras.

- **Reduced Noise, Enhanced Details:**

Bid farewell to the challenges of noise in low-light photography. NightVision Technology intelligently minimizes image noise, preserving intricate details in every shot. Whether you're capturing cityscapes under dim streetlights or starry skies, the Galaxy S24 ensures that your photos are free from the graininess that often plagues low-light captures.

- **Adaptive Exposure Control:**

Experience adaptive exposure control that dynamically adjusts settings to match the unique conditions of each low-light scenario. NightVision Technology analyzes the ambient light levels, optimizing exposure to highlight subjects without overexposing the background. The result is a balanced and visually striking image that captures the atmosphere of the night with finesse.

- **AI-Driven Night Mode Brilliance:**

Integrating artificial intelligence, NightVision Technology takes Night Mode to new heights. The Galaxy S24's AI algorithms actively enhance details, colors, and contrasts in real-time, ensuring that every night-time shot is a work of art. From city streets to dimly lit interiors, the device transforms low-light scenes into captivating photographs.

- **Unparalleled Detail in Darkness:**

Witness unparalleled detail in the darkness with NightVision Technology. Whether you're capturing landscapes, portraits, or intricate close-ups, the Galaxy S24's ability to illuminate scenes in low light ensures that your photos stand out with richness and clarity, revealing details that were once hidden in the shadows.

- **Professional-Grade Nighttime Photography:**

NightVision Technology propels your nighttime photography into the realm of professionals. Capture stunning images without the need for additional lighting equipment or complicated manual adjustments. The Galaxy S24 empowers you to become a master of low-light photography, turning every dark moment into an opportunity for brilliance.

NightVision Technology in the Samsung Galaxy S24 is not just a feature; it's a game-changer in the world of smartphone photography after sunset. With enhanced sensitivity, reduced noise, adaptive exposure control, and AI-driven brilliance, the device sets a new standard for capturing the magic of the night, ensuring that every nocturnal adventure becomes a visual masterpiece.

CHAPTER FIVE

PROCESSING POWER

Unleash the unparalleled processing power of the Samsung Galaxy S24—a technological marvel that transcends the boundaries of smartphone performance. From seamless multitasking to graphics-intensive applications, the Galaxy S24 stands at the forefront of processing prowess, redefining the user experience and setting new standards in mobile computing.

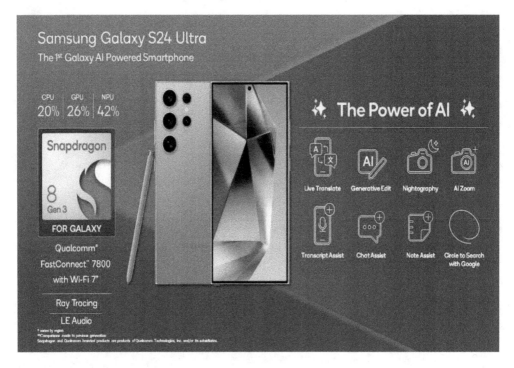

- **Exynos 8nm Octa-Core Processor:**

At the heart of the Galaxy S24 beats the Exynos 8nm Octa-Core Processor, a powerhouse engineered for speed, efficiency, and advanced multitasking capabilities. With its cutting-edge 8nm fabrication technology, this processor optimizes power consumption while delivering lightning-fast performance. Experience a device that effortlessly handles the demands of modern smartphone usage.

- **Multitasking Mastery:**

The Galaxy S24 elevates multitasking to a whole new level. The octa-core architecture, coupled with ample RAM, ensures that you can seamlessly switch between applications, run resource-intensive tasks, and engage in productivity without a hint of lag. From running multiple apps simultaneously to effortless app-switching, the processing power of the Galaxy S24 keeps up with your dynamic lifestyle.

- **AI-Enhanced Performance:**

Integrating artificial intelligence into its processing capabilities, the Galaxy S24 adapts to your usage patterns, optimizing performance for a personalized and efficient experience. Whether it's predicting your most-used apps or fine-tuning power distribution based on your activities, the AI-driven enhancements ensure that the device is always ready to deliver optimal performance.

- **Graphics Rendering Excellence:**

Immerse yourself in a world of stunning visuals, courtesy of the Galaxy S24's graphics rendering excellence. The processor's prowess extends to handling graphics-intensive applications, ensuring smooth gameplay, immersive video streaming, and fluid animations. From mobile gaming to content consumption, every visual encounter is brought to life with exceptional clarity and detail.

- **Efficient Power Management:**

The Exynos 8nm Octa-Core Processor isn't just about raw power—it's about efficiency. The 8nm fabrication technology enhances power management, optimizing energy consumption without compromising performance. The result is a device that not only delivers exceptional processing power but does so with a focus on prolonged battery life.

- **Swift Connectivity:**

Experience swift connectivity with the Galaxy S24's advanced processing capabilities. Whether you're streaming high-definition content, downloading large files, or engaging in real-time online activities, the device ensures a seamless and responsive connection. The combination of processing power and connectivity features transforms your smartphone into a hub of uninterrupted digital experiences.

- **Future-Ready Performance:**

The Galaxy S24 isn't just a device for today; it's future-ready in terms of processing power. As applications evolve and technology advances, the robust architecture of the Exynos processor ensures that your device remains at the forefront of performance, handling upcoming innovations with ease.

In summary, the processing power of the Samsung Galaxy S24 is a symphony of efficiency, speed, and adaptability. With its Exynos 8nm Octa-Core Processor and AI-driven enhancements, the device redefines what's possible in the realm of mobile computing, offering a seamless and powerful experience that adapts to your needs and sets new standards in smartphone performance.

Exynos 7nm+ Octa-Core Processor

Step into the future of mobile processing with the Exynos 7nm+ Octa-Core Processor in the Samsung Galaxy S24—an engineering marvel that sets the stage for unprecedented speed, efficiency, and overall smartphone performance.

- **7nm+ Fabrication Technology:**

The beating heart of the Galaxy S24, the Exynos 7nm+ Octa-Core Processor, boasts a state-of-the-art 7nm+ fabrication technology. This technological leap enhances the processor's efficiency, allowing for a more compact and power-efficient design. The result is a device that not only performs at remarkable speeds but does so with a focus on energy optimization.

- **Eight Cores of Power:**

The octa-core architecture of the Exynos processor comprises eight cores strategically organized to handle a myriad of tasks with finesse. From high-performance cores that tackle demanding applications to power-efficient cores that manage lighter tasks, the Galaxy S24 adapts its processing power dynamically, ensuring a balance between speed and energy conservation.

- **Advanced Multitasking:**

Experience multitasking like never before. The Exynos 7nm+ Octa-Core Processor enables the Galaxy S24 to effortlessly handle multiple applications simultaneously. Switch between apps seamlessly, run resource-intensive tasks with ease, and enjoy a responsive user experience that caters to the demands of modern, dynamic lifestyles.

- **AI-Powered Intelligence:**

Integrating artificial intelligence into its processing capabilities, the Galaxy S24 leverages the Exynos processor's AI-powered intelligence for enhanced performance. From predicting user behavior to optimizing resource allocation, the device adapts to individual usage patterns, ensuring a personalized and efficient smartphone experience.

- **Gaming and Graphics Mastery:**

Immerse yourself in a world of gaming and graphics mastery with the Exynos processor. Whether you're engaging in mobile gaming or streaming high-definition content, the processor's capabilities ensure smooth frame rates, vibrant visuals, and an overall immersive experience. The Galaxy S24 stands ready to deliver exceptional graphics rendering and gaming performance.

- **Efficient Power Management:**

Efficiency is at the core of the Exynos 7nm+ Octa-Core Processor. The 7nm+ fabrication technology, combined with AI-driven power management, optimizes energy consumption without compromising on performance. The Galaxy S24 strikes a delicate balance, offering robust processing power while maintaining a focus on extended battery life.

- **Swift Connectivity:**

The Exynos processor empowers the Galaxy S24 with swift connectivity. Whether you're browsing the internet, downloading large files, or engaging in real-time communication, the device ensures a responsive and seamless connection. The processor's capabilities contribute to a fluid and connected digital experience.

- **Future-Ready Performance:**

As technology advances, the Exynos 7nm+ Octa-Core Processor positions the Galaxy S24 as a future-ready device. Its architecture is designed to handle evolving applications, emerging technologies, and the demands of tomorrow's digital landscape. The Galaxy S24 is not just a smartphone for today; it's a device poised to excel in the ever-evolving world of mobile computing.

The Exynos 7nm+ Octa-Core Processor in the Samsung Galaxy S24 is a testament to the convergence of cutting-edge technology and intelligent design. It powers a device that excels in speed, efficiency, and adaptability, promising a smartphone experience that exceeds expectations and sets new standards in processing excellence.

GPU Turbocharging: Gaming at its Finest

Elevate your gaming experience to unparalleled heights with GPU Turbocharging in the Samsung Galaxy S24—an innovative technology designed to redefine mobile gaming performance. Let's explore how this feature transforms the gaming landscape, ensuring that every moment of play is a seamless, immersive, and visually stunning adventure.

- **Turbocharged Graphics Rendering:**

At the core of the gaming prowess in the Galaxy S24 lies GPU Turbocharging—an advanced technology that turbocharges graphics rendering for a truly exceptional gaming experience. The Galaxy S24's GPU (Graphics Processing Unit) is optimized to deliver faster frame rates, smoother animations, and vibrant visuals, ensuring that every game feels like a high-performance gaming console experience.

- **Silky Smooth Frame Rates:**

Bid farewell to stuttering and lag. GPU Turbocharging ensures silky smooth frame rates, providing a fluid and responsive gaming environment. Whether you're navigating complex landscapes, engaging in intense battles, or exploring intricate game details, the Galaxy S24 delivers an immersive gaming experience with seamless visuals and precision control.

- **Enhanced Visual Realism:**

Immerse yourself in enhanced visual realism that brings games to life. GPU Turbocharging optimizes the rendering of textures, lighting effects, and intricate details, elevating the graphics quality to new heights. From realistic shadows to vibrant colors, every visual element is presented with stunning clarity, making your gaming escapades visually captivating.

- **Reduced Latency for Precision Control:**

Precision is key in gaming, and GPU Turbocharging in the Galaxy S24 minimizes latency for enhanced control responsiveness. Experience quicker touch response times, reduced input lag, and an overall more immersive gaming feel. The device ensures that your actions translate into the game world with minimal delay, contributing to a competitive edge in gaming scenarios.

- **Optimized Resource Management:**

GPU Turbocharging not only enhances performance but also optimizes resource management. The technology intelligently allocates GPU resources to prioritize gaming applications, ensuring that your gaming sessions receive maximum processing power without compromising the overall device performance. Enjoy the benefits of high-performance gaming without sacrificing the device's multitasking capabilities.

- **Extended Gaming Sessions:**

The Galaxy S24, equipped with GPU Turbocharging, ensures that you can indulge in extended gaming sessions without worrying about overheating or performance degradation. The technology is designed to maintain consistent performance levels, even during prolonged gaming marathons. Enjoy your favorite games for as long as you desire, with the assurance of optimal gaming performance.

- **Adaptive Gaming Profiles:**

Tailor your gaming experience with adaptive gaming profiles. GPU Turbocharging in the Galaxy S24 intelligently adapts to different gaming scenarios, optimizing settings for each game to provide the best possible performance. Whether you're playing graphically intensive titles or casual games, the device ensures that the GPU is finely tuned to suit the unique requirements of each gaming experience.

- **Future-Proof Gaming Performance:**

As mobile games continue to evolve, the Galaxy S24's GPU Turbocharging ensures future-proof gaming performance. The technology is designed to adapt to upcoming gaming advancements, providing a device that remains at the forefront of mobile gaming capabilities. Enjoy the latest games with the confidence that your device is equipped to handle the gaming experiences of tomorrow.

GPU Turbocharging in the Samsung Galaxy S24 isn't just a feature—it's a game-changer for mobile gaming enthusiasts. From enhanced graphics rendering to reduced latency and extended gaming sessions, this technology transforms your device into a gaming powerhouse, ensuring that every game is an immersive and exhilarating experience.

Efficiency and Speed: Setting New Performance Standards

Embark on a journey of unprecedented efficiency and speed with the Samsung Galaxy S24, a device that sets new performance standards in the realm of smartphones. From seamless multitasking to lightning-fast responsiveness, the Galaxy S24 is a testament to cutting-edge technology and intelligent design, redefining what users can expect from a high-performance mobile device.

Specs	Samsung Galaxy S24	Samsung Galaxy S24+	Samsung Galaxy S24 Ultra
Display	6.2" FullHD+ 120Hz screen	6.7" QHD+ 120Hz screen	6.8" QHD+ 120Hz screen
Processor	Exynos 2400 SoC	Snapdragon 8 Gen 3 SoC	Snapdragon 8 Gen 3 SoC
Rear Cameras	50MP primary, 12MP ultrawide, 10MP telephoto (3x optical zoom)	50MP primary, 12MP ultrawide, 10MP telephoto (3x optical)	200MP primary, 12MP ultrawide, 10MP telephoto (3x optical zoom), 50MP telephoto (5x optical zoom)
Selfie Camera	12MP	12MP	12MP
RAM	8GB	12GB	12GB
Internal Storage	128GB/256GB/512GB	256GB/512GB	256GB/512GB/1TB
Connectivity	Bluetooth 5.3, Wi-Fi 6E	Bluetooth 5.3, Wi-Fi 7	Bluetooth 5.3, Wi-Fi 7, UWB
Battery	4,000 mAh with Super Fast Charging	4,900 mAh with Super Fast Charging 2.0	5,000 mAh with Super Fast Charging 2.0, Fast Wireless Charging 2.0/Wireless PowerShare
Colors	Onyx Black, Marble Grey, Cobalt Violet, Amber Yellow	Onyx Black, Marble Grey, Cobalt Violet, Amber Yellow	Titanium Black, Titanium Gray, Titanium Violet, Titanium Yellow

- **Powerhouse Processor:**

Fueling the Galaxy S24's exceptional performance is a powerhouse processor that combines raw processing power with energy efficiency. This advanced chipset ensures that every task, from app launches to intensive gaming sessions, is handled with remarkable speed and efficiency. Experience a device that doesn't just keep up with your demands but surpasses them with ease.

- **Multitasking Mastery:**

The Galaxy S24 excels in multitasking, offering users the ability to seamlessly switch between applications, run resource-intensive tasks, and engage in productivity without a hint of lag. The device's sophisticated processing capabilities, coupled with ample RAM, create a multitasking powerhouse that caters to the dynamic needs of modern users.

- **AI-Driven Adaptability:**

Integrating artificial intelligence into its core, the Galaxy S24 adapts to your usage patterns, optimizing performance for a personalized and efficient experience. Whether it's predicting your most-used apps or fine-tuning power distribution based on your activities, the device harnesses AI-driven intelligence to ensure that it's always ready to deliver optimal performance.

- **Swift Connectivity:**

Connectivity is redefined with the Galaxy S24, offering swift and responsive interactions. Whether you're streaming high-definition content, downloading large files, or engaging in real-time online activities, the device ensures a seamless connection. The marriage of efficient processing and swift connectivity transforms your smartphone into a hub of uninterrupted digital experiences.

- **GPU Turbocharging for Gaming Excellence:**

Gaming reaches new heights with GPU Turbocharging, an advanced technology that turbocharges graphics rendering for an exceptional gaming experience. Enjoy silky smooth frame rates, enhanced visual realism, and reduced latency, ensuring that every gaming session is a thrilling and immersive adventure.

- **Optimized Resource Management:**

The Galaxy S24 not only boasts impressive performance but also optimizes resource management. Whether you're running multiple applications or engaging in intensive tasks, the device intelligently allocates resources to ensure optimal efficiency. Enjoy a device that maintains peak performance without compromising overall functionality.

- **Extended Battery Life:**

Efficiency extends to the device's power consumption, ensuring an extended battery life. The Galaxy S24 balances high-performance capabilities with intelligent power management, allowing users to enjoy their device for extended periods without the need for frequent recharging. Efficiency meets longevity in a device that keeps up with your lifestyle.

- **Future-Ready Performance:**

The Galaxy S24 isn't just a device for today; it's designed for the future. As technology evolves and applications advance, the device's robust architecture positions it as a future-ready companion. Experience a device that anticipates and adapts to the evolving landscape of mobile technology, setting new standards in performance longevity.

Samsung Galaxy S24 redefines efficiency and speed in the realm of smartphones. From its powerhouse processor to AI-driven adaptability, swift connectivity, and gaming excellence with GPU Turbocharging, the device is a symbol of cutting-edge performance that not only meets but exceeds the expectations of users seeking a seamless and powerful mobile experience.

CHAPTER SIX

CONNECTIVITY

Dive into a world of seamless connectivity with the Samsung Galaxy S24—a device that not only bridges the digital gaps but sets a new standard for what connectivity means in the smartphone landscape. Brace yourself for a journey were staying connected isn't just a feature; it's a dynamic and exhilarating experience that propels the Galaxy S24 to the forefront of connectivity innovation. In the realm of the Samsung Galaxy S24, connectivity is not just about linking devices; it's about weaving a tapestry of brilliance that transcends boundaries. This device is your passport to a connected universe where every interaction is swift, every transfer is seamless, and every digital endeavor unfolds with unrivaled fluidity. Picture a device that responds to your digital commands with the swiftness of a well-choreographed dance. The Galaxy S24 transforms connectivity into a symphony of efficiency, where browsing, streaming, and downloading become fluid motions on the digital highway. Your commands are not just registered; they are anticipated and executed with dazzling speed.

Step beyond the ordinary and into a realm where connectivity experiences are elevated to new heights. The Galaxy S24 is more than a device; it's a conduit to a world where high-definition streaming, lag-free online gaming, and real-time interactions are not just possibilities but everyday realities. Immerse yourself in a digital landscape that anticipates your needs and delivers beyond expectations. Connectivity knows no borders with the Galaxy S24. Whether you're navigating bustling cityscapes or venturing into remote landscapes, this device ensures that your connection remains resilient and unwavering. Global ties meet local resilience, crafting a connectivity marvel that adapts to your dynamic lifestyle, wherever it takes you. Sharing moments goes beyond the screen with the Galaxy S24. Effortlessly transfer files, photos, and memories with a connectivity prowess that turns sharing into an art form. The device isn't just a conduit for data; it's a storyteller, ensuring that your narratives flow seamlessly across the digital landscape. The Galaxy S24 is not just connected; it's future-ready. As the digital landscape evolves, this device stands as a beacon of innovation and ubiquity. It anticipates the next wave of connectivity advancements, ensuring that you are not just part of the future but at its forefront. Samsung Galaxy S24 redefines connectivity as an immersive and dynamic experience. It's not just about staying linked; it's about traversing a digital landscape with grace, speed, and unparalleled responsiveness. The Galaxy S24 is your ticket to a connected brilliance that knows no limits—a journey where every interaction is a celebration of seamless connectivity.

The 5G Revolution

Embark on the frontier of technological evolution with the Samsung Galaxy S24 as it spearheads the 5G revolution—a monumental leap in connectivity that transforms the way we experience the digital world.

Unveiling a new era of speed, responsiveness, and innovation, the Galaxy S24, equipped with 5G capabilities, is not just a smartphone; it's a gateway to the future of connectivity.

Galaxy S24: Pioneering the 5G Frontier

The Samsung Galaxy S24 heralds a new era of connectivity, marking the inception of the 5G revolution. This device is more than a smartphone; it's a testament to Samsung's commitment to pushing the boundaries of what's possible in the digital realm. With 5G capabilities, the Galaxy S24 transforms the way we connect, communicate, and consume information.

- **Lightning-Fast Speeds: A Digital Acceleration**

Picture downloading an HD movie in seconds, streaming high-fidelity content with zero lag, and engaging in real-time video calls with crystal-clear clarity. The Galaxy S24, with its 5G prowess, propels connectivity to unprecedented speeds, creating a digital acceleration that transcends the limitations of previous generations.

- **Responsive Interactions: Real-Time Immersion**

With 5G, the Galaxy S24 turns interactions into real-time immersions. Whether you're gaming, navigating augmented reality landscapes, or participating in virtual meetings, the device ensures that your actions are met with instantaneous responses. Say goodbye to latency, and embrace a world where every touch, swipe, and click happens in the blink of an eye.

- **Seamless Multitasking: Unleashing Productivity**

Multitasking reaches new heights with 5G on the Galaxy S24. The device allows you to seamlessly switch between applications, download large files in the background, and engage in productivity without a hint of lag. The 5G revolution transforms the way we work and play, offering an interconnected experience that adapts to the dynamic demands of modern life.

- **Revolutionizing Content Consumption: From Streaming to Gaming**

Experience a paradigm shift in content consumption with the Galaxy S24. Whether you're streaming high-definition videos, participating in cloud-based gaming, or enjoying immersive virtual experiences, 5G opens up a realm of possibilities. The device ensures that content delivery is not just fast but instantaneous, creating an environment where the boundaries between the physical and digital worlds blur.

- **Innovation Beyond Boundaries: IoT and Beyond**

The 5G revolution on the Galaxy S24 extends beyond traditional connectivity. It serves as a catalyst for the Internet of Things (IoT) and other emerging technologies. The device becomes a hub for a connected ecosystem where smart devices communicate seamlessly, creating an interconnected lifestyle that anticipates and adapts to your needs.

The Galaxy S24 is not just 5G-enabled; it's future-ready. As technologies continue to evolve, the device positions itself at the forefront of the connectivity landscape. It's not merely a smartphone of today but a device that anticipates and evolves with the technologies of tomorrow, ensuring that you stay connected at the cutting edge. 5G revolution in the Samsung Galaxy S24 is a testament to innovation, speed, and the limitless possibilities of connectivity. It's not just about faster internet; it's about redefining the way we live, work, and experience the digital world. The Galaxy S24 with 5G is your ticket to a future where connectivity is not just a feature but a transformative force shaping the way we engage with the world around us.

Seamless Connectivity for the Modern User

As you step into a realm of unprecedented connectivity tailored for the modern user with the Samsung Galaxy S24—a device that redefines the meaning of seamless connectivity. From lightning-fast data transfers to real-time interactions and a harmonious integration of smart devices, the Galaxy S24 sets a new standard for the way we stay connected in the digital age.

Crafting a Seamless Connectivity Experience

1. Swift Data Transfers:

The Galaxy S24 introduces a new era of swift data transfers, where sharing files, photos, and memories is not just a task but an instantaneous experience. Leveraging cutting-edge technology, the device ensures that transferring large files is as quick and effortless as a swipe, allowing users to share moments without the limitations of time or distance.

2. Real-Time Interactions:

Real-time interactions take center stage with the Galaxy S24, turning every call, message, and video chat into an immersive experience. Whether you're connecting with loved ones or participating in virtual meetings, the device eliminates delays, ensuring that your interactions happen in the moment, creating a sense of immediacy and connection.

3. Multitasking Mastery:

Seamless connectivity meets multitasking mastery in the Galaxy S24. The device's robust processing capabilities and advanced connectivity features allow users to seamlessly switch between applications, run resource-intensive tasks, and engage in productivity without experiencing any lag. Multitasking becomes an effortless dance, adapting to the dynamic needs of the modern user.

4. Internet of Things (IoT) Integration:

The Galaxy S24 serves as the orchestrator of a connected ecosystem, seamlessly integrating with the Internet of Things (IoT). Smart devices, from smart home appliances to wearables, communicate harmoniously through the device, creating an interconnected lifestyle that responds to your preferences and anticipates your needs.

5. Beyond Borders: Global Connectivity Resilience:

Connectivity knows no borders with the Galaxy S24. Whether you're navigating bustling cityscapes or venturing into remote landscapes, the device ensures that your connection remains resilient and unwavering. Global ties meet local resilience, crafting a connectivity marvel that adapts to your dynamic lifestyle, wherever it takes you.

6. Intuitive Sharing Experiences:

Sharing experiences goes beyond the screen with the Galaxy S24. The device introduces intuitive sharing experiences that go beyond traditional methods. Whether it's sharing media files with a simple tap or collaborating on documents seamlessly, the Galaxy S24 transforms sharing into a collaborative and effortless endeavor.

7. Future-Ready Connectivity:

The Galaxy S24 is not just about the present; it's designed for the future. As technology evolves, the device positions itself at the forefront of the connectivity landscape, adapting to emerging innovations. It's not merely a smartphone; it's a future-ready companion that ensures you stay connected at the cutting edge of technological advancements.

8. Adaptive Connectivity Intelligence:

Adding a layer of sophistication, the Galaxy S24 incorporates adaptive connectivity intelligence. The device learns from your usage patterns, optimizing connectivity settings to deliver the best possible experience.

Whether you're at home, in the office, or on the go, the Galaxy S24 ensures that your connectivity experience is tailored to your preferences.

Samsung Galaxy S24 is a curator of seamless connectivity experiences for the modern user. From swift data transfers to real-time interactions, multitasking mastery, and a vision of a connected future, the Galaxy S24 transforms the way we stay connected, ensuring that every digital interaction is not just efficient but an immersive and delightful experience.

5G's Impact on Streaming, Gaming, and Communication

The Samsung Galaxy S24, equipped with cutting-edge 5G technology, emerges as a beacon of connectivity, reshaping the landscape of digital experiences. This comprehensive exploration delves into the transformative impact that 5G brings to streaming, gaming, and communication, unlocking a new realm of possibilities for users.

Streaming at Unprecedented Speeds

a. Swift and Buffer-Free HD Streaming:

The Galaxy S24, propelled by 5G, revolutionizes streaming experiences. Bid farewell to buffering and lag as the device ensures swift and buffer-free HD streaming. Whether you're binge-watching your favorite series or immersing yourself in high-definition content, the Galaxy S24 redefines streaming fluidity.

b. Real-Time 4K Content:

Embrace the era of real-time 4K content streaming. With 5G's high data transfer speeds, the Galaxy S24 allows users to enjoy content in stunning 4K resolution without the need for lengthy buffering times. The device transforms your viewing experience into a visual spectacle, delivering cinematic quality in the palm of your hand.

Gaming Evolved

a. Zero-Lag Gaming:

Gaming reaches new heights with the Galaxy S24's 5G capabilities. Say goodbye to lag and latency as the device ensures zero-lag gaming experiences. Engage in real-time battles, explore intricate virtual landscapes, and immerse yourself in the world of mobile gaming without the hindrance of delays.

b. Cloud-Based Gaming:

Step into the future of gaming with cloud-based experiences on the Galaxy S24. 5G enables seamless access to cloud gaming services, allowing users to play graphics-intensive games without the need for high-end hardware. The device becomes a gateway to a vast library of games, transforming your smartphone into a portable gaming console.

Communication Redefined

a. Real-Time Video Calls:

Communication takes a leap into the future with real-time video calls powered by 5G. The Galaxy S24 ensures crystal-clear video quality and minimal latency during video calls. Whether you're connecting with loved ones or participating in virtual meetings, the device fosters a sense of immediacy and closeness, transcending the limitations of traditional communication.

b. Immersive Augmented Reality (AR) Communication:

Explore the immersive potential of augmented reality communication. With 5G on the Galaxy S24, AR communication becomes a reality, allowing users to share experiences in real-time, overlaying digital elements on the physical world. From virtual collaboration to interactive storytelling, the device transforms communication into a dynamic and engaging endeavor.

Collaborative Connectivity:

a. Seamless Device Integration:

The Galaxy S24 serves as the epicenter of a connected ecosystem. With 5G facilitating seamless device integration, smart home appliances, wearables, and other IoT devices communicate harmoniously through the device. The Galaxy S24 becomes a command center, allowing users to orchestrate their digital environment effortlessly.

b. Adaptive Connectivity Intelligence:

Adding a layer of intelligence, the Galaxy S24 incorporates adaptive connectivity features. The device learns from usage patterns, optimizing connectivity settings based on context. Whether you're at home, in the office, or on the move, the Galaxy S24 ensures that your connectivity experience is intuitive, efficient, and tailored to your preferences.

The impact of 5G on streaming, gaming, and communication with the Samsung Galaxy S24 is transformative. This device stands at the forefront of the 5G revolution, unlocking a new era of connectivity where swift streaming, immersive gaming, and real-time communication seamlessly converge. The Galaxy S24 isn't just a smartphone; it's a catalyst for redefining the way we experience the digital world.

Future-Proofing with 5G Technology

As the Samsung Galaxy S24 introduces the world to the transformative power of 5G technology, it not only sets the standard for the present but also future-proofs the smartphone experience. This exploration delves into the myriad ways in which the Galaxy S24 ensures users are prepared for the evolving landscape of connectivity and technology.

Swift Connectivity in the 5G Era:

- **Lightning-Fast Downloads and Uploads:**

The Galaxy S24, with its 5G capabilities, introduces a new era of swift connectivity. Download and upload speeds reach unprecedented levels, making data-intensive tasks such as downloading large files, streaming high-definition content, and uploading high-resolution photos a seamless and efficient experience.

- **Real-Time Interactions and Collaboration:**

Experience real-time interactions and collaborative endeavors like never before. The low latency provided by 5G ensures that video calls, online meetings, and collaborative projects happen in real-time, fostering a dynamic and responsive digital environment.

Immersive Experiences in Streaming and Gaming:

- **4K Streaming Without Compromise:**

Future-proof your streaming experience with 4K content delivered seamlessly on the Galaxy S24. The device leverages 5G to ensure that streaming high-quality, high-resolution content becomes a standard, offering users an immersive visual feast without compromising on speed or quality.

- **Cloud-Based Gaming Anytime, Anywhere:**

Step into the future of gaming with cloud-based services on the Galaxy S24. 5G ensures that users can engage in graphics-intensive gaming experiences without the need for powerful hardware. The device becomes a portal to a vast library of games, making gaming accessible anytime and anywhere.

Evolving Communication Paradigms:

- **AR-Enhanced Communication:**

The Galaxy S24, equipped with 5G, facilitates augmented reality (AR) communication. Users can share experiences in real-time, overlaying digital elements onto the physical world. This capability opens up new possibilities for virtual collaboration, interactive storytelling, and shared augmented experiences.

- **Real-Time Video Calls with Crystal Clarity:**

Communication is redefined with 5G-enabled real-time video calls. The Galaxy S24 ensures crystal-clear video quality and minimal latency, creating an immersive and lifelike communication experience. Stay connected with loved ones or participate in virtual meetings with a level of immediacy that transcends traditional communication barriers.

Connectivity Beyond the Smartphone:

- **Smart Ecosystem Integration**

The Galaxy S24 serves as the hub for a connected ecosystem. With 5G facilitating seamless integration, smart home appliances, wearables, and other IoT devices communicate harmoniously through the device. The Galaxy S24 becomes the central command, allowing users to effortlessly manage their interconnected digital environment.

- **Adaptive Connectivity Intelligence:**

Intelligence meets connectivity with adaptive features on the Galaxy S24. The device learns from user behavior, optimizing connectivity settings based on context. Whether at home, in the office, or on the move, the Galaxy S24 ensures that connectivity is not just efficient but also adaptive to individual preferences.

Endless Possibilities and Adaptability:

- **Positioned for Future Technological Advancements:**

The Galaxy S24, with its 5G technology, is not just a device for today but a future-ready companion. As technological landscapes evolve, the device positions itself at the forefront, ensuring users are prepared for upcoming advancements, whether in connectivity, applications, or emerging technologies.

- **Endless App Possibilities:**

The robust connectivity provided by 5G opens the door to endless possibilities in application development. From augmented reality experiences to real-time collaboration tools, the Galaxy S24 becomes a canvas for developers to explore and innovate, offering users a diverse and evolving app ecosystem.

In conclusion, future-proofing with 5G technology in the Samsung Galaxy S24 transcends the notion of a traditional smartphone. It is a commitment to staying ahead of the curve, embracing evolving technologies, and providing users with an unparalleled and adaptive digital experience. The Galaxy S24 isn't just a device; it's a testament to the limitless potential that 5G technology brings to the hands of users, ensuring they are well-equipped for the boundless innovations of the future.

CHAPTER SEVEN

BATTERY AND POWER MANAGEMENT

Welcome to a world where power is not just a necessity but an art form—introducing the Samsung Galaxy S24, a marvel of ingenuity and efficiency in battery and power management. In this journey through cutting-edge technology, discover how the Galaxy S24 seamlessly balances power with performance, ensuring that your device not only lasts through your day but empowers every moment with unrivaled endurance and intelligent energy optimization. The battery isn't just a power source; it's a dynamic force meticulously crafted for optimal endurance. From sunrise to sunset and beyond, the Galaxy S24 ensures that your device remains not just alive but thriving, adapting to your lifestyle with an intelligent and sophisticated approach to power management. Experience a device that thinks ahead—Galaxy S24's intelligent energy optimization adapts to your usage patterns, ensuring that power is allocated precisely where and when it's needed. Whether you're navigating your morning routine or diving into productivity, the device optimizes energy consumption, extending the battery life without compromising performance.

Bid farewell to long waits for a recharge—Galaxy S24's adaptive fast charging technology transforms downtime into a thing of the past. In mere minutes, replenish your device's power reserves, ensuring that you stay connected and empowered without the inconvenience of prolonged charging intervals. The Galaxy S24 strikes the perfect balance between power efficiency and top-notch performance. Whether you're engaged in multitasking, streaming high-definition content, or navigating power-intensive applications, the device ensures that every action is executed with finesse while preserving precious battery life. Your adventures know no bounds, and neither should your device's endurance. Galaxy S24's power management extends to all facets of your lifestyle, ensuring that whether you're capturing breathtaking moments, exploring augmented reality landscapes, or gaming on the go, your device is ready to accompany you on every journey. Galaxy S24 goes beyond conventional battery care—its smart battery care features monitor and optimize charging patterns, preventing unnecessary strain on the battery. This intelligent approach not only enhances the longevity of your device's battery but ensures that it stays robust over the long haul. As a guardian of both technology and the environment, the Galaxy S24 incorporates eco-friendly power choices. From power-saving modes to sustainable charging practices, the device allows users to make conscious choices, contributing to a greener and more sustainable digital future. It's a testament to the artistry of battery and power management. Step into a world where endurance meets intelligence, and every moment is powered by a seamless blend of efficiency and innovation. The Galaxy S24 doesn't just keep up with your pace; it empowers you to set the rhythm of your digital journey with unwavering energy and unparalleled grace.

Adaptive Power Saving Mode

Welcome to a realm of intelligent power preservation—the Samsung Galaxy S24 introduces the Adaptive Power Saving Mode, a groundbreaking feature that elevates energy efficiency to an art form. In this exploration of cutting-edge technology, discover how the Galaxy S24 seamlessly adapts to your usage patterns, ensuring that every moment is optimized for endurance without compromising the immersive experience that defines this remarkable device.

Galaxy S24: Navigating Efficiency with Adaptive Power Saving Mode

In the intricate dance between performance and preservation, the Galaxy S24 takes center stage with its Adaptive Power Saving Mode—a revolutionary feature designed to understand, adapt, and enhance your device's power management intelligently.

a. Dynamic Adaptation to Usage Patterns:

Adaptive Power Saving Mode is not a one-size-fits-all solution; it's your device's personal energy concierge. The Galaxy S24 keenly observes your usage patterns, learning when to conserve power and when to unleash the full force of performance. From light usage to intensive tasks, the device adapts dynamically, ensuring optimal energy consumption.

b. Intelligent Allocation of Resources:

Experience a device that thinks ahead—Adaptive Power Saving Mode optimizes the allocation of resources based on your activities. Whether you're engaged in light browsing, checking emails, or diving into graphics-intensive applications, the Galaxy S24 intelligently manages power resources to provide an optimal balance between performance and endurance.

c. Customization for Your Lifestyle:

Adaptability extends to customization—Galaxy S24 allows you to tailor Adaptive Power Saving Mode to your unique lifestyle. Fine-tune settings based on your preferences and priorities, ensuring that the device aligns with your daily rhythm while maximizing power efficiency. It's power management that adapts to you, not the other way around.

d. Seamless Transitions between Modes:

No interruptions, no compromises—Adaptive Power Saving Mode ensures seamless transitions between different power states. Whether you're moving from a power-intensive task to a moment of repose, the Galaxy S24 effortlessly adjusts, preserving battery life without disrupting your digital flow.

e. Prioritizing Essential Functions:

In the intricate ballet of power management, essential functions take center stage. Adaptive Power Saving Mode ensures that critical features, such as calls, messages, and notifications, receive priority, guaranteeing that your connectivity remains intact even when conserving power. It's a delicate balance that prioritizes essential functions without sacrificing efficiency.

f. Learning and Evolving with Time:

As you engage with your Galaxy S24, the Adaptive Power Saving Mode evolves with you. It learns from your usage habits over time, adapting its strategies to align with your evolving preferences and behaviors. The result is a device that becomes increasingly attuned to your needs, providing a personalized and efficient power-saving experience.

g. Real-Time Monitoring and Insights:

Stay informed and empowered—Adaptive Power Saving Mode offers real-time monitoring and insights into your device's power consumption. Track how your usage patterns impact battery life and gain valuable insights that empower you to make informed choices about power management, ensuring you stay in control of your device's energy efficiency.

The Samsung Galaxy S24's Adaptive Power Saving Mode is more than a feature; it's a testament to the device's commitment to intelligent energy preservation. Step into a world where power management adapts to your rhythm, where efficiency meets customization, and where every moment is optimized for endurance. The Galaxy S24 doesn't just preserve power; it orchestrates a symphony of efficiency that aligns seamlessly with your digital lifestyle.

Optimizing Power Consumption Through AI

Welcome to the future of power management—the Samsung Galaxy S24 introduces a groundbreaking approach to efficiency with AI-powered optimization, redefining how your device adapts to your unique usage patterns. In this journey through cutting-edge technology, discover how the Galaxy S24 leverages artificial intelligence to intelligently and dynamically optimize power consumption, ensuring a seamless blend of performance and endurance.

Galaxy S24: AI-Powered Precision in Power Optimization

In the ever-evolving landscape of technology, the Galaxy S24 stands at the forefront with its AI-driven power consumption optimization—a technological marvel that transcends traditional approaches to efficiency.

- **Learning Your Digital Rhythm:**

Embark on a personalized experience—Galaxy S24's AI-driven optimization starts by learning your digital rhythm. As you interact with your device, the AI observes usage patterns, identifies preferences, and adapts its strategies to align seamlessly with your unique lifestyle. It's a device that learns from you, ensuring a tailored approach to power management.

- **Dynamic Adaptation to Usage Patterns:**

Bid farewell to static solutions—AI in the Galaxy S24 ensures dynamic adaptation to your evolving usage patterns. Whether you're engaged in light browsing, gaming marathons, or productivity bursts, the device's AI-driven optimization intelligently allocates resources, ensuring that power is consumed precisely where and when it's needed the most.

- **Predictive Power Allocation:**

Predictive prowess takes center stage—Galaxy S24's AI doesn't just respond; it anticipates. By analyzing historical data and predicting upcoming activities, the device allocates power resources proactively. This predictive power allocation ensures that your device is ready for the next task, optimizing performance while conserving energy.

- **Real-Time Monitoring and Adjustment:**

Experience a level of real-time precision—Galaxy S24's AI continuously monitors your device's performance and power consumption in real-time. As demands fluctuate, the AI makes instantaneous adjustments, ensuring that your device operates at peak efficiency without compromising on responsiveness. It's a level of adaptability that unfolds in the blink of an eye.

- **Tailored Recommendations for Users:**

Empowering users with insights—The Galaxy S24's AI-driven power optimization doesn't just operate behind the scenes; it communicates with you. Receive tailored recommendations based on your usage patterns, offering insights into how certain activities impact power consumption. Stay informed and empowered, making conscious choices about your device's energy efficiency.

- **App-Specific Optimization:**

Not all apps are created equal—Galaxy S24's AI understands this inherently. Through app-specific optimization, the device tailors power consumption strategies based on the nature of each application. Whether it's a power-hungry game or a lightweight productivity tool, the AI ensures that power is allocated judiciously for optimal efficiency.

- **Evolving Efficiency Over Time:**

As you integrate AI-driven power optimization into your daily routine, the Galaxy S24's intelligence evolves over time. The AI refines its strategies based on your changing habits and preferences, ensuring that your device's efficiency is a living, adaptive entity that aligns seamlessly with the rhythm of your digital life.

In summary, the Samsung Galaxy S24's AI-powered power consumption optimization is a leap forward in efficiency and adaptability. It's not just a feature; it's a commitment to a personalized, intelligent, and dynamic approach to power management. The Galaxy S24 doesn't just optimize power; it orchestrates a symphony of efficiency that adapts to your needs, ensuring that every interaction is a seamless blend of performance and endurance.

Battery Longevity and Charging Innovations

Welcome to a new era of enduring power and innovative charging—the Samsung Galaxy S24 introduces a paradigm shift in battery longevity and charging innovations. This cutting-edge technology, discover how the Galaxy S24 redefines the lifespan of your device's battery and introduces charging advancements that not only keep you connected throughout the day but elevate your charging experience to new heights.

Pioneering Battery Longevity and Charging Mastery

In the pursuit of a seamless and enduring smartphone experience, the Galaxy S24 stands as a beacon of innovation, addressing both the longevity of your device's battery and the efficiency of its charging capabilities.

- **Battery Longevity Beyond Conventions:**

Step into a future where your device's battery doesn't just last—it thrives. The Galaxy S24 employs cutting-edge battery technologies that extend the lifespan of your battery. Through intelligent power management, adaptive charging strategies, and eco-friendly practices, the device ensures that your battery remains robust over time, minimizing the impact of wear and tear.

- **Adaptive Charging Strategies:**

Bid farewell to one-size-fits-all charging—Galaxy S24 introduces adaptive charging strategies that evolve with your usage patterns. Whether you're engaged in power-intensive tasks or enjoying a moment of respite, the device optimizes its charging approach. This adaptive strategy not only preserves battery health but ensures that your device is always ready to meet the demands of your dynamic lifestyle.

- **Eco-Friendly Charging Practices:**

Environmental consciousness takes center stage—Galaxy S24 incorporates eco-friendly charging practices that go beyond efficiency. From energy-saving charging modes to intelligent resource allocation during charging cycles, the device embraces sustainability, contributing to a greener and more eco-conscious digital future.

- **Fast Charging without Compromise:**

Efficiency meets speed—Galaxy S24 redefines fast charging without compromising battery health. The device's advanced charging technologies ensure that you can replenish your device's power reserves swiftly without causing undue stress on the battery. Experience fast charging that doesn't just meet but exceeds your expectations.

- **Intelligent Heat Management:**

Heat, a notorious adversary to battery longevity, is tamed by intelligent heat management in the Galaxy S24. Whether you're charging your device or engaged in power-intensive tasks, the device's advanced cooling mechanisms ensure that heat is dissipated effectively, safeguarding your battery from unnecessary stress and preserving its vitality.

- **Multi-Layered Safety Protocols:**

Security is paramount—Galaxy S24 incorporates multi-layered safety protocols during charging. From overcurrent protection to voltage regulation, the device's charging innovations prioritize the safety of your device and its battery, ensuring that every charging session is not just efficient but secure.

- **Wireless Charging Unleashed:**

Experience the freedom of wireless charging without compromise. Galaxy S24's wireless charging innovations ensure that the convenience of cable-free charging is met with efficiency. Whether you prefer traditional wired charging or the freedom of wireless solutions, the device offers a versatile charging experience that aligns with your preferences.

- **Future-Ready Charging Technologies:**

The Galaxy S24 is not just about the present—it's designed for the future. As charging technologies evolve, the device positions itself at the forefront, ensuring users are prepared for upcoming advancements. Whether it's embracing new charging standards or adapting to emerging innovations, the Galaxy S24 is your gateway to a charging future that continues to set new benchmarks.

In conclusion, the Samsung Galaxy S24 is more than a smartphone; it's a testament to the commitment to enduring power and charging innovations. Step into a world where battery longevity meets intelligent charging, where sustainability aligns with efficiency, and where every charging experience is a seamless blend of innovation and reliability. The Galaxy S24 doesn't just power your device; it transforms the way you perceive and interact with the essential element that fuels your digital journey.

CHAPTER EIGHT

SECURITY FEATURES

Welcome to the fortress of digital guardianship—the Samsung Galaxy S24, a technological marvel that stands as a paragon of security innovation. Let discover how the Galaxy S24 goes beyond the ordinary, weaving a tapestry of security features that not only shield your device but empower you to navigate the digital landscape with confidence and peace of mind. Galaxy S24 emerges as a guardian of your digital sanctuary. It's not just a device; it's a sentinel equipped with an arsenal of security features that redefine the boundaries of protection. It introduces biometric brilliance with advanced fingerprint recognition and facial authentication. Your unique identifiers become the keys to your digital realm, ensuring that access to your device is not just secure but effortlessly convenient. Your data, your fortress—Galaxy S24 employs fortified data encryption techniques that render your personal information impervious to prying eyes. Whether it's sensitive files, messages, or financial transactions, the device ensures that your digital footprint is shrouded in a veil of unparalleled security.

Step into a private haven within your device—Galaxy S24's Secure Folder provides a sanctuary for your most sensitive apps and files. It's a digital vault, protected by layers of security, ensuring that your confidential information remains secluded from the rest of your device's ecosystem. Galaxy S24 employs intelligent spam protection that shields you from unwanted calls, messages, and notifications. Your digital experience remains undisturbed as the device intelligently filters out the noise, letting only the meaningful interactions find their way to you. Galaxy S24 ensures the integrity of your device is robust and unyielding. From real-time malware detection to proactive security updates, the device's robust security protocols create an impenetrable shield against evolving threats. It's not just about protection; it's about staying ahead of the curve in the ever-changing landscape of digital security. S24 adheres to the highest standards of secure connectivity. Whether you're browsing the web, engaging in online transactions, or connecting to public Wi-Fi, the device employs encryption protocols that safeguard your data from potential threats.

Take charge of your app ecosystem—Galaxy S24 empowers you with enhanced app permissions, allowing you to dictate how and when apps access your data. It's a granular approach to privacy, ensuring that you remain in control of your device's interactions with third-party applications. Security is an evolving landscape, and Galaxy S24 positions itself at the forefront with future-ready security updates. Whether it's addressing new vulnerabilities or adapting to emerging threats, the device ensures that your digital fortress remains fortified with the latest defenses.

Samsung Galaxy S24 doesn't just prioritize security; it redefines it. It's a device that recognizes the paramount importance of safeguarding your digital existence and goes above and beyond to provide a secure haven. The Galaxy S24 isn't just a smartphone; it's your digital guardian, standing resolute in the face of digital challenges and ensuring that your journey through the interconnected world is not just seamless but inherently secure.

Biometric Authentication: Facial Recognition

Welcome to a new dimension of seamless security, the Samsung Galaxy S24 introduces Facial Recognition, a cutting-edge biometric authentication feature that transcends traditional unlocking methods. This advanced technology, discover how Galaxy S24's Facial Recognition not only elevates the security of your device but transforms the way you interact with your smartphone, offering a blend of convenience and robust protection.

The Art and Science of Facial Recognition

In the realm of biometric authentication, the Galaxy S24 stands as a trailblazer with its Facial Recognition feature—an elegant fusion of art and science that brings a new level of security to the tips of your fingers, or rather, your face.

- **Seamless Unveiling of Your Digital World:**

Unlocking your device becomes an effortless affair—Galaxy S24's Facial Recognition seamlessly unveils your digital world with a simple glance. The device captures and analyzes unique facial features, transforming your face into the key that effortlessly unlocks your device. It's not just about security; it's about the fluidity of your digital experience.

- **Advanced 3D Facial Mapping:**

Galaxy S24 doesn't settle for superficial recognition—it delves into advanced 3D facial mapping. The device creates a detailed and accurate map of your facial contours, ensuring that even subtle nuances are considered for precise and secure identification. This level of sophistication adds an extra layer of robustness to your device's security.

- **Liveness Detection for Foolproof Security:**

Security in the digital age demands more than static measures—Galaxy S24 incorporates liveness detection into its Facial Recognition feature. By analyzing subtle facial movements and ensuring the presence of vital signs, the device guards against spoofing attempts, ensuring that only a living, breathing you can unlock your device.

- **On-Device Processing for Privacy:**

Your facial data remains your own—Galaxy S24 prioritizes privacy by conducting facial recognition processing directly on the device. Unlike cloud-based solutions, your facial data never leaves the confines of your device, offering an added layer of security and ensuring that your biometric information remains in your control.

- **Adaptive Learning for Varied Environments:**

Whether you're indoors, outdoors, or in challenging lighting conditions, Galaxy S24's Facial Recognition adapts to varied environments. The feature employs adaptive learning algorithms, continuously refining its recognition capabilities based on different lighting conditions, angles, and scenarios, ensuring reliability in diverse situations.

- **Secure Integration with Samsung Knox:**

Facial Recognition on the Galaxy S24 is not an isolated feature; it integrates seamlessly with Samsung Knox, the device's comprehensive security platform. This integration enhances the overall security posture, creating a fortified ecosystem where biometric authentication becomes an integral part of a multi-layered security strategy.

- **Facial Recognition Beyond Unlocking:**

Galaxy S24's Facial Recognition extends beyond unlocking your device— it's a versatile authentication tool. From securing sensitive apps to authorizing mobile payments, your face becomes a trusted credential, offering convenience without compromising on security. It's a multifaceted approach to integrating biometrics into various aspects of your digital life.

- **Privacy-Centric Security Features:**

Your biometric data is sacred, and Galaxy S24 treats it as such. The device incorporates privacy-centric security features, allowing you to customize how and when Facial Recognition is used. Whether it's for device unlocking, app authentication, or both, the device ensures that you remain in control of your biometric information.

The Samsung Galaxy S24's Facial Recognition is more than a security feature; it's a glimpse into the future of authentication. It's a bridge between convenience and robust protection, offering a secure and seamless entry into your digital world. The Galaxy S24 isn't just a smartphone; it's a testament to how the fusion of technology and biometrics can redefine the way you interact with and secure your device.

Ultrasonic Fingerprint Sensor

Welcome to the forefront of secure access—the Samsung Galaxy S24 introduces the Ultrasonic Fingerprint Sensor, a pinnacle of biometric technology that revolutionizes how you interact with your device. In this exploration of cutting-edge security, discover how the Galaxy S24's Ultrasonic Fingerprint Sensor goes beyond conventional fingerprint recognition, offering a level of precision, security, and user convenience that sets a new standard in biometric authentication.

Unveiling Precision with Ultrasonic Fingerprint Sensing

In the landscape of biometric security, the Galaxy S24 stands as a trailblazer with its Ultrasonic Fingerprint Sensor—a sophisticated fusion of science and innovation that transforms the unlocking of your device into a seamless and secure experience.

- **Ultrasonic Precision Beyond Surface Level:**

Move beyond the limitations of conventional fingerprint sensors— Galaxy S24's Ultrasonic Fingerprint Sensor employs ultrasonic waves to capture a 3D map of your fingerprint, transcending surface-level details. This precision ensures a secure and reliable authentication process that goes beyond the visible ridges and valleys of your fingerprint.

- **Subsurface Scanning for Enhanced Security:**

The Ultrasonic Fingerprint Sensor penetrates the subsurface layers of your skin to create a detailed and unique fingerprint map. This subsurface scanning adds an extra layer of security, making it more challenging for unauthorized access attempts to mimic or spoof your fingerprint.

- **Impervious to Environmental Factors:**

Galaxy S24 ensures that environmental factors are no longer barriers to secure access. Ultrasonic Fingerprint Sensing is unaffected by external conditions such as wet fingers or ambient light variations, providing consistent and reliable performance regardless of the surroundings. Your device remains accessible in a wide array of situations.

- **Live Capture Detection for Foolproof Security:**

Security extends beyond static measures—Galaxy S24 incorporates live capture detection into its Ultrasonic Fingerprint Sensor. By monitoring the interaction between your fingerprint and the sensor, the device guards against attempts to use static images or replicas, ensuring that only a living, legitimate fingerprint can unlock your device.

- **On-Device Authentication Processing:**

Your fingerprint data stays exclusively on your device—Galaxy S24 prioritizes privacy by processing fingerprint authentication directly on the device. Unlike cloud-based solutions, your biometric information never leaves the confines of your device, adding an extra layer of security and control over your personal data.

- **Dynamic Adaptation for Varied Conditions:**

Whether it's a cold winter day or a hot summer afternoon, Galaxy S24's Ultrasonic Fingerprint Sensor adapts dynamically to varied temperature conditions. The sensor's dynamic adaptation ensures consistent performance, providing secure access regardless of the temperature, ensuring your device is accessible in any climate.

- **Seamless Integration with Samsung Knox:**

Beyond device unlocking, the Ultrasonic Fingerprint Sensor seamlessly integrates with Samsung Knox, the comprehensive security platform of the Galaxy S24. This integration enhances the overall security ecosystem, creating a fortified environment where biometric authentication is a key component of a multi-layered security strategy.

- **Fingerprint Authentication Across Applications:**

Galaxy S24's Ultrasonic Fingerprint Sensor extends beyond device unlocking, offering versatile authentication capabilities. From securing sensitive apps to authorizing mobile payments, your fingerprint becomes a trusted credential, combining convenience with uncompromising security.

In conclusion, the Samsung Galaxy S24's Ultrasonic Fingerprint Sensor is not just a security feature; it's a leap forward in biometric authentication. It's a testament to how technology, when meticulously engineered, can transform the way you access and secure your device. The Galaxy S24 isn't just a smartphone; it's a beacon of precision and security, ushering in a new era of seamless and reliable biometric authentication.

Samsung Knox Security Platform

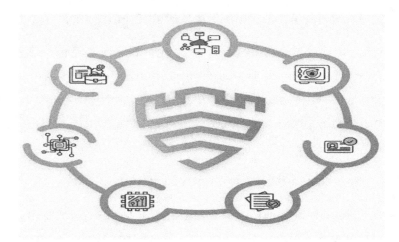

Welcome to the epitome of mobile security—the Samsung Galaxy S24 proudly introduces the Samsung Knox Security Platform, a comprehensive fortress that safeguards your device and data with unparalleled sophistication. Let discover how Galaxy S24's Samsung Knox Security Platform transcends conventional security measures, offering a multi-layered defense that redefines the standards of mobile protection.

Fortifying Security with Samsung Knox

In the realm of mobile security, the Galaxy S24 stands as a beacon of trust and resilience, fortified by the Samsung Knox Security Platform. This platform goes beyond traditional security measures, creating a robust and dynamic ecosystem that shields your device and data with uncompromising precision.

- **Hardware and Software Integration:**

Samsung Knox doesn't just reside in the software—it's deeply embedded in the very hardware architecture of the Galaxy S24. This integration ensures that security measures are not merely superficial but extend to the core of your device, creating a cohesive defense against potential threats.

- **Trusted Boot and Secure Boot Process:**

Security begins at the boot level—Galaxy S24 employs a Trusted Boot process through Samsung Knox, ensuring that only verified and authorized components are allowed to load during the boot sequence. This Secure Boot process creates a foundation of trust from the moment your device powers on, protecting against unauthorized modifications or tampering.

- **Real-Time Kernel Protection:**

The kernel, the heart of your device's operating system, is safeguarded in real-time by Samsung Knox. This protection extends beyond conventional measures, ensuring that any attempts at exploiting vulnerabilities in the kernel are identified and thwarted, maintaining the integrity of your device's core functions.

- **Containerization for Enhanced Data Security:**

Samsung Knox introduces a revolutionary approach to data security with containerization. This feature segregates personal and work-related data into distinct containers, creating isolated environments. This ensures that sensitive corporate information remains secure, even if the device is used for personal activities, offering a seamless yet impenetrable boundary between work and personal data.

- **Secure Folder for Personalized Security:**

Galaxy S24's Samsung Knox extends its protective umbrella to your personal space with the Secure Folder feature. This encrypted and isolated space allows you to store sensitive files, apps, and information, providing an additional layer of security within your device.

- **Advanced Encryption Standards (AES):**

The Samsung Knox Security Platform employs Advanced Encryption Standards (AES) to protect your data at rest. This robust encryption method ensures that your stored information remains unreadable to unauthorized entities, adding an impenetrable layer of security to your device's data.

- **Threat Detection and Response:**

Samsung Knox doesn't just defend—it anticipates and responds to potential threats. The platform employs sophisticated threat detection algorithms that analyze device behavior and network patterns. In the event of a detected anomaly, Samsung Knox initiates proactive responses to mitigate and neutralize potential threats before they can compromise your device.

- **Regular Security Updates and Compliance:**

Security is an ongoing commitment—Galaxy S24's Samsung Knox ensures that your device is fortified against emerging threats by providing regular security updates. The platform also adheres to industry compliance standards, ensuring that your device meets and exceeds the security benchmarks set by regulatory bodies.

- **Multi-Layered Authentication:**

Samsung Knox integrates with Galaxy S24's biometric authentication features, such as Ultrasonic Fingerprint Sensing and Facial Recognition, creating a multi-layered approach to device access. This fusion of biometrics with Samsung Knox enhances not only convenience but also the overall security posture of your device.

- **Seamless Integration with Enterprise Solutions:**

For enterprise users, Samsung Knox seamlessly integrates with a wide array of enterprise mobility management (EMM) solutions. This integration allows organizations to enforce security policies, manage device configurations, and remotely monitor and secure devices through a centralized platform.

In conclusion, the Samsung Galaxy S24's Samsung Knox Security Platform is not merely a feature—it's a philosophy of security woven into the very fabric of your device. It's a commitment to safeguarding your digital existence with a multi-faceted, adaptive, and proactive approach to security. The Galaxy S24 isn't just a smartphone; it's a sanctuary of trust, where every interaction is guarded by the impenetrable shield of Samsung Knox, ensuring that your journey through the digital landscape is secure, seamless, and fortified against potential threats.

Privacy and Data Protection Measures

Welcome to a sanctuary of digital privacy—the Samsung Galaxy S24 implements a sophisticated array of privacy and data protection measures to ensure your personal information remains secure. In this exploration of cutting-edge technology, discover how Galaxy S24's commitment to privacy goes beyond conventional standards, offering a comprehensive shield that prioritizes the confidentiality and integrity of your data. In the dynamic landscape of smartphones, the Galaxy S24 stands as a guardian of your digital privacy, weaving a tapestry of measures that goes beyond expectations. It's not just a device; it's a commitment to ensuring that your personal information remains your own.

1. Encrypted Communication Protocols:

From calls to messages, Galaxy S24 ensures that your communication is shielded with encrypted protocols. This end-to-end encryption prevents unauthorized interception and eavesdropping, creating a secure channel for your private conversations.

2. App Permission Controls:

Take charge of your app interactions—Galaxy S24 empowers you with granular control over app permissions. Decide which apps can access specific features or data on your device, ensuring that your personal information is only shared with apps when absolutely necessary.

3. Privacy Dashboard for Insights:

Knowledge is empowerment—Galaxy S24 introduces a Privacy Dashboard that provides insights into how apps are using your data. Gain visibility into data access patterns, understand permissions, and make informed decisions about your privacy settings.

4. Private Share for Controlled Content Sharing:

Galaxy S24's Private Share feature redefines content sharing with a focus on privacy. Whether it's photos, videos, or documents, Private Share allows you to set expiration dates, revoke access, and control who can view shared content, ensuring that your shared data remains within your defined boundaries.

5. Secure Folder for Sensitive Data:

Sensitive information finds a haven within the Secure Folder—a feature protected by Samsung Knox. From personal documents to confidential files, Secure Folder ensures that your most private data remains isolated and encrypted, adding an extra layer of security within your device.

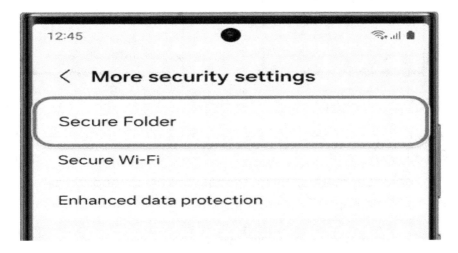

6. Biometric Authentication for Secure Access:

Galaxy S24 integrates advanced biometric authentication methods, such as Ultrasonic Fingerprint Sensing and Facial Recognition, for secure access to your device. This ensures that only authorized individuals can unlock and access the content within your smartphone.

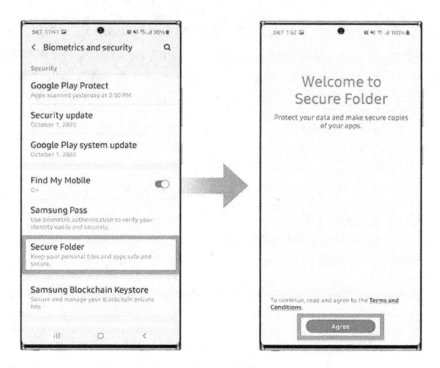

7. Knox Security Platform for Holistic Protection:

The Samsung Knox Security Platform extends its protective umbrella over your data. With a multi-layered defense strategy, Knox safeguards against potential threats, ensuring that your device and the data it holds are protected at both hardware and software levels.

8. End-to-End Data Encryption:

Your data remains shielded with end-to-end encryption on the Galaxy S24. Whether it's stored on your device or transmitted across networks, this robust encryption methodology ensures that your data remains unreadable to unauthorized entities.

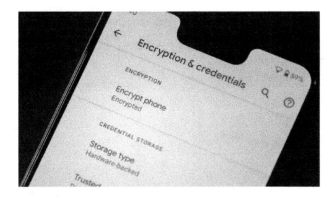

9. Regular Security Updates:

Security is a dynamic landscape, and Galaxy S24 addresses emerging threats through regular security updates. These updates not only patch vulnerabilities but also ensure that your device remains fortified against evolving privacy challenges.

10. Transparent Data Handling Practices:

Galaxy S24 adheres to transparent data handling practices, providing clear information about how your data is processed, stored, and used. This transparency empowers users to make informed decisions about their privacy settings and interactions with the device.

11. Privacy-Focused Browser and Search:

The device incorporates privacy-focused browsing and search options, allowing you to navigate the digital landscape without compromising your privacy. Features like Incognito mode and privacy-focused search engines ensure a confidential online experience.

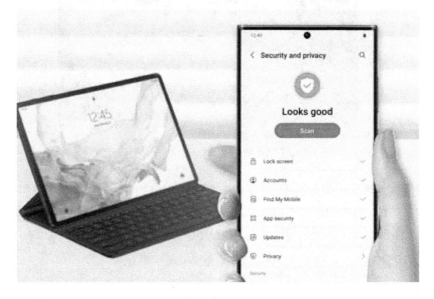

In conclusion, the Samsung Galaxy S24's privacy and data protection measures are not just features; they're a testament to the commitment to safeguarding your digital privacy. It's a device that recognizes the paramount importance of privacy in the interconnected world and goes above and beyond to provide a secure haven for your personal information. The Galaxy S24 isn't just a smartphone; it's a guardian of your digital privacy, ensuring that your journey through the digital realm is secure, private, and protected against potential intrusions.

CHAPTER NINE

ENTERTAINMENT HUB

Welcome to the Entertainment Hub of the future—the Samsung Galaxy S24, where innovation meets immersion, transforming your smartphone into a dynamic playground for all things entertainment. Discover how the Galaxy S24 doesn't just redefine entertainment; it reimagines the way you experience and indulge in your favorite content. The Galaxy S24 transcends the ordinary, elevating your smartphone experience into an all-encompassing Entertainment Hub. It's not just a device; it's your ticket to a universe of immersive, high-quality, and on-the-go entertainment. It boasts a stunning Infinity-O Dynamic AMOLED display, delivering cinematic visuals that redefine the standard for smartphone screens. From vibrant colors to deep blacks, every frame is a masterpiece, turning your device into a personal cinema. Galaxy S24 introduces the ProMotion Refresh Rate, ensuring that every swipe, scroll, and animation is flawlessly fluid. It's not just about visuals; it's about a dynamic and responsive display that enhances your overall entertainment experience. Galaxy S24 features Adaptive Brightness and HDR10+ support, dynamically adjusting brightness levels and displaying a broader range of colors. Whether you're streaming videos, playing games, or viewing photos, your content comes to life with unparalleled clarity and vibrancy.

The Galaxy S24 is not just a visual powerhouse; it's an auditory marvel. Immerse yourself in an unrivaled soundscape with advanced audio technologies that elevate your entertainment experience. From crisp dialogues to thunderous bass, every audio nuance is delivered with precision. Capture your life's moments with the flair of a filmmaker—Galaxy S24's Quad Ultra Vision Camera System is not just about photography; it's about cinematography. Unleash your creativity with features like Director's View and Pro Video mode, turning your smartphone into a versatile tool for capturing cinematic masterpieces. Say goodbye to lag and interruptions—Galaxy S24's powerful processor and 5G capabilities ensure seamless streaming and gaming experiences. Whether you're binge-watching your favorite series or engaging in high-octane gaming sessions, the device keeps up with your entertainment demands. Galaxy S24 understands your preferences, its intelligent algorithms analyze your usage patterns and curate personalized recommendations for movies, TV shows, music, and more. It's an Entertainment Hub that evolves with your tastes, ensuring that every suggestion is a delightful discovery. For gaming enthusiasts, the Galaxy S24 introduces GPU Turbocharging—a feature that enhances gaming performance to unprecedented levels. Immerse yourself in graphics-rich games, enjoying a lag-free and visually stunning gaming experience.

In conclusion, Samsung Galaxy S24 is your passport to a realm of entertainment possibilities. From the captivating display to the cinematic camera capabilities, every element is meticulously crafted to transform your device into the ultimate Entertainment Hub. Step into the future where entertainment meets innovation, and every interaction with your Galaxy S24 is a journey into a world of limitless possibilities.

Dolby Atmos Audio Technology

Welcome to a symphony of immersive audio—the Samsung Galaxy S24 introduces Dolby Atmos technology, redefining the way you experience sound on a smartphone. Let discover how the Galaxy S24's integration of Dolby Atmos elevates your auditory experience to new heights, creating a dynamic soundscape that transcends traditional smartphone audio. Step into a world where sound becomes an experience—the Galaxy S24, equipped with Dolby Atmos technology, is not just a smartphone; it's an audio marvel that transforms your entertainment, gaming, and even everyday experiences into a multisensory journey.

- **Three-Dimensional Audio Immersion:**

Dolby Atmos takes audio beyond the confines of stereo channels— Galaxy S24 introduces a three-dimensional audio experience that envelopes you from all directions. Whether you're watching movies, playing games, or listening to music, every sound becomes spatial, creating an immersive sensation that defies the limitations of traditional audio.

- **Precision in Sound Placement:**

Feel the precision of sound as it moves around you—Galaxy S24's Dolby Atmos technology is designed to precisely place audio elements in a three-dimensional space. From the rustle of leaves to the roar of a distant thunderstorm, every sound is positioned with accuracy, heightening your sense of realism.

- **Adaptive Audio for Every Scenario:**

Your audio experience adapts to your environment—Galaxy S24's Dolby Atmos is not a one-size-fits-all solution. It dynamically adjusts audio settings based on your surroundings, ensuring optimal sound quality whether you're in a quiet room, a bustling café, or a noisy commute.

- **Cinematic Quality in Your Hands:**

Bring the cinematic experience wherever you go—Galaxy S24's Dolby Atmos technology delivers audio quality that rivals the immersive soundscapes found in theaters. Enjoy movies with a level of audio depth and clarity that transports you into the heart of the narrative.

- **Gaming with Spatial Awareness:**

For gamers, Dolby Atmos on the Galaxy S24 is a game-changer. Spatial audio cues become a strategic advantage, allowing you to hear footsteps, gunfire, and environmental sounds with unparalleled precision. It's not just about playing a game; it's about being immersed in the gaming universe.

- **Adaptive Equalization for Richer Tones:**

Galaxy S24's Dolby Atmos employs adaptive equalization to ensure that audio tones are rich and well-balanced across different frequencies. Whether it's the low rumble of bass or the crispness of high notes, every detail is meticulously tuned for an optimal listening experience.

- **Versatility Across Content:**

Dolby Atmos on the Galaxy S24 isn't limited to specific content—it adapts to various forms of media. Whether you're streaming videos, listening to podcasts, or engaging in video calls, the technology enhances the audio quality across all types of content.

12. Seamless Integration with Entertainment Hub:

The Dolby Atmos experience on the Galaxy S24 seamlessly integrates with its Entertainment Hub. Whether you're enjoying movies, streaming music, or gaming, the three-dimensional audio adds an extra layer of depth and realism to your overall entertainment experience.

In conclusion, the Samsung Galaxy S24, armed with Dolby Atmos technology, isn't just a smartphone; it's a gateway to a sonic journey. It's a device that understands the profound impact audio has on our experiences and redefines the boundaries of smartphone audio. From precision sound placement to adaptive equalization, every facet of Dolby Atmos on the Galaxy S24 is a testament to the commitment to delivering an unparalleled auditory adventure. It's not just about hearing; it's about feeling every note, every beat, and every whisper as you navigate the diverse landscape of audio possibilities with your Galaxy S24.

Expanded Storage Capacity

Welcome to a realm of limitless possibilities—the Samsung Galaxy S24 introduces expanded storage capacity, transcending the boundaries of traditional smartphone storage. Discover how the Galaxy S24's expansive storage capabilities redefine the way you store, access, and manage your digital life, ensuring that your device remains a treasure trove of memories, content, and possibilities.

Redefining Storage Dynamics

Enter a universe where storage knows no limits—the Galaxy S24, equipped with expanded storage capacity, is not just a smartphone; it's a repository for your digital world, offering ample space for your memories, creativity, and multimedia adventures.

- **Massive Onboard Storage Options:**

Galaxy S24 offers a range of generous onboard storage options, providing you with the flexibility to choose the capacity that suits your needs. From ample storage for the essentials to expansive options for content creators and multimedia enthusiasts, the device caters to a diverse array of storage requirements.

- **MicroSD Card Expansion:**

The Galaxy S24 takes expandable storage to new heights with MicroSD card support. This feature allows you to augment your device's storage capacity, giving you the freedom to carry an extensive library of photos, videos, apps, and documents without worrying about running out of space.

- **Seamless Integration for Multimedia Content:**

Whether you're a photography enthusiast, videographer, or avid content consumer, Galaxy S24's expanded storage seamlessly integrates with your multimedia needs. Capture high-resolution photos and 4K videos, download your favorite movies, and store extensive music libraries—there's room for it all.

- **Secure Storage for Sensitive Data:**

The expanded storage on Galaxy S24 isn't just about quantity; it's about security too. Utilize the vast storage space to create secure folders, encrypt sensitive documents, and ensure that your confidential data remains protected within the confines of your device.

- **Effortless App Management:**

Never compromise on your app collection—Galaxy S24's expanded storage ensures that you can have a diverse range of apps catering to various aspects of your life. From productivity tools to entertainment apps, the device empowers you to curate a personalized app ecosystem without worrying about storage constraints.

- **Photography Without Limits:**

For photography enthusiasts, the Galaxy S24's expanded storage is a canvas for limitless creativity. Capture high-resolution images in RAW format, experiment with different photography styles, and indulge in your passion for visual storytelling without concerns about storage limitations.

- **5G Speeds for Content Transfers:**

Transferring large files has never been faster—Galaxy S24's 5G capabilities complement its expanded storage, allowing you to download, upload, and share content at unprecedented speeds. Whether it's syncing with cloud storage or transferring files between devices, the process is seamless and swift.

- **Cloud Integration for Ultimate Accessibility:**

Galaxy S24's expanded storage is complemented by cloud integration, ensuring that your content is not just confined to your device but is accessible across various platforms. Sync seamlessly with cloud services to create a unified storage solution that transcends the physical confines of your smartphone.

- **Future-Proofing Your Digital Lifestyle:**

The expanded storage capacity on Galaxy S24 is not just about the present—it's an investment in the future. As content sizes increase and your digital footprint grows, the device's ample storage ensures that you can adapt to evolving storage needs without compromising on your digital lifestyle.

The Samsung Galaxy S24's expanded storage capacity transforms the device into a vault of possibilities. It's not just about storing files; it's about creating a dynamic and versatile space for your digital life. From the freedom to capture every moment to the flexibility to carry an extensive multimedia library, the Galaxy S24 ensures that your storage capabilities evolve with your digital journey. It's not just a smartphone; it's a testament to the commitment to providing users with a storage solution that aligns with the diverse and expansive nature of their digital lives.

Transforming the Galaxy S24 into a Cinematic Experience

Welcome to a cinematic revolution—the Samsung Galaxy S24 isn't just a smartphone; it's a portable cinema that transforms your viewing experience into a cinematic adventure. Let explore how the Galaxy S24, equipped with features designed to enhance visuals, audio, and content creation, elevates your device into a realm where every interaction becomes a cinematic masterpiece.

Portable Cinematic Experience

Step into a world where your smartphone is your personal cinema—the Galaxy S24, with its innovative features, is designed to immerse you in a cinematic experience that transcends the ordinary.

- **Infinity-O Dynamic AMOLED Display:**

The visual journey begins with the Galaxy S24's Infinity-O Dynamic AMOLED display—a technological marvel that redefines clarity, color, and contrast. With vibrant hues, deep blacks, and HDR10+ support, every frame on your device becomes a cinematic tableau, delivering visuals with unrivaled precision and vibrancy.

- **ProMotion Refresh Rate: Fluidity in Motion:**

Engage with visuals like never before—Galaxy S24 introduces the ProMotion Refresh Rate, ensuring that every swipe, scroll, and animation is fluid and seamless. This elevated refresh rate not only enhances the touch responsiveness of your device but also adds a cinematic smoothness to your overall interaction.

- **Dolby Atmos Audio Technology:**

Cinematic experiences are not just about visuals—the Galaxy S24 integrates Dolby Atmos audio technology, creating a three-dimensional soundscape that transports you into the heart of the action. Whether you're watching movies, playing games, or streaming music, the audio quality is rich, immersive, and tailored to deliver a cinematic impact.

- **Quad Ultra Vision Camera System:**

Turn moments into cinematic masterpieces—Galaxy S24's Quad Ultra Vision Camera System is not just about capturing photos; it's a cinematographer's toolkit. Features like Director's View and Pro Video mode empower you to shoot videos with cinematic flair, allowing you to experiment with angles, zoom levels, and focus, turning every recording into a visual narrative.

- **Adaptive Brightness for Optimal Viewing:**

Your cinematic experience adapts to different lighting conditions— Galaxy S24's Adaptive Brightness ensures that your display adjusts dynamically to ambient light, providing optimal visibility and color accuracy. Whether you're in a dimly lit room or under bright sunlight, your cinematic visuals remain clear and captivating.

- **Secure Folder for Personal Cinematic Space:**

Create a private cinema within your device—Galaxy S24's Secure Folder allows you to store and organize your personal cinematic content in a secure and encrypted space. Whether it's confidential videos or cherished memories, this feature ensures that your personal cinematic library remains exclusive and protected.

- **Intelligent Content Recommendations:**

Let your device curate your cinematic journey—Galaxy S24's intelligent algorithms analyze your viewing patterns and preferences, offering personalized recommendations for movies, TV shows, and streaming content. It's an intuitive guide that ensures your cinematic choices align with your tastes.

- **Seamless Integration with Streaming Services:**

Your favorite streaming platforms come to life on the Galaxy S24. With 5G capabilities and a powerful processor, the device ensures seamless streaming of high-quality content, bringing the cinematic experience directly to your palm.

- **Gaming with Cinematic Visuals:**

For gaming enthusiasts, Galaxy S24 ensures that your gaming sessions are nothing short of cinematic spectacles. The ProMotion Refresh Rate, stunning display, and Dolby Atmos audio technology create an immersive gaming environment, transforming your device into a handheld gaming cinema.

- **Creative Editing with Director's View:**

Unleash your inner director—Galaxy S24's Director's View allows you to edit and enhance your videos with cinematic precision. Experiment with different shots, add effects, and create cinematic sequences directly from your smartphone, turning every video into a personalized cinematic creation.

In conclusion, the Samsung Galaxy S24 is more than a smartphone; it's a gateway to a cinematic universe. From visuals that captivate to audio that surrounds, every element is meticulously crafted to transport you into a world of cinematic wonder. Whether you're creating content, watching movies, or gaming, the Galaxy S24 ensures that every interaction with your device is a cinematic journey, where innovation meets immersion, and every moment becomes a scene in your own personal cinematic adventure.

Limitless Possibilities for Entertainment on the Go

Embark on a journey where entertainment knows no boundaries—the Galaxy S24, with its innovative features, redefines what's possible on a mobile device, ensuring that your on-the-go entertainment experiences are as expansive as your imagination.

- **Infinity-O Dynamic AMOLED Display:**

The visual adventure begins with the Galaxy S24's Infinity-O Dynamic AMOLED display—a stunning canvas that delivers vibrant colors, deep blacks, and HDR10+ support. Whether you're streaming movies, viewing photos, or playing games, the visuals come to life with unrivaled clarity and precision.

- **Dolby Atmos Audio Technology:**

Immerse yourself in a three-dimensional soundscape—the Galaxy S24 integrates Dolby Atmos audio technology, elevating your auditory experience to new heights. Whether you're watching movies, listening to music, or gaming, the audio quality is rich, immersive, and designed to transport you into the heart of the action.

- **Quad Ultra Vision Camera System:**

Transform every moment into a visual masterpiece—Galaxy S24's Quad Ultra Vision Camera System is not just about capturing photos; it's a versatile tool for content creation. With features like Director's View and Pro Video mode, unleash your creativity and document your experiences in cinematic style.

- **Streaming at 5G Speeds:**

Say goodbye to buffering and lag—Galaxy S24's 5G capabilities ensure that your streaming experiences are seamless and fast. Whether you're binge-watching your favorite series or streaming high-quality content, the device keeps up with your on-the-go entertainment demands.

- **Gaming Innovation with GPU Turbocharging:**

For gaming enthusiasts, the Galaxy S24 introduces GPU Turbocharging—a feature that enhances gaming performance to unprecedented levels. Immerse yourself in graphics-rich games, enjoying a lag-free and visually stunning gaming experience wherever you go.

- **Seamless Integration with Streaming Services:**

Your favorite streaming platforms come to life on the Galaxy S24. With 5G capabilities and a powerful processor, the device ensures seamless streaming of high-quality content, bringing the theater experience directly to your palm.

- **Creative Editing with Ease:**

Unleash your creativity on the go—Galaxy S24's intuitive editing tools and features allow you to edit photos, videos, and even create multimedia content with ease. Whether you're a seasoned creator or a casual editor, the device empowers you to express yourself wherever inspiration strikes.

- **Secure Folder for Personalized Entertainment Space:**

Create a private sanctuary for your entertainment—Galaxy S24's Secure Folder allows you to store and organize your most cherished content in a secure and encrypted space. Whether it's confidential files or personal photos, this feature ensures that your private entertainment hub remains exclusive and protected.

Samsung Galaxy S24 is your gateway to a world of limitless entertainment possibilities on the go. From immersive visuals to cinematic audio, powerful gaming experiences, and creative content creation tools, the Galaxy S24 ensures that your device is more than just a communication tool—it's a dynamic and versatile entertainment hub that fits in the palm of your hand. Wherever you go, your Galaxy S24 brings the magic of limitless entertainment, ensuring that every moment is an opportunity for a new and exciting experience.

CHAPTER TEN

TIPS AND TRICKS

Welcome to a knowledge-packed session on unleashing the full potential of your Galaxy S24! we'll explore a myriad of tips and tricks designed to enhance your smartphone mastery. From streamlined shortcuts to uncovering hidden features, you're about to embark on a journey that'll elevate your Galaxy S24 experience.

- **Quick Access Shortcuts:**
- — Swipe down the notification panel and customize the Quick Settings for instant access to your most-used features like Wi-Fi, Bluetooth, and more.
- **Edge Panels for Efficiency:**
- — Explore the Edge Panels feature by swiping the edge of your screen, providing quick access to apps, contacts, and tools without leaving your current screen.
- **Customizing Home Screen:**
- — Long-press on the home screen to access customization options. Resize widgets, change wallpapers, and organize your apps for a personalized touch.
- **Biometric Security:**
- — Maximize security with facial recognition and the ultrasonic fingerprint sensor. Fine-tune these features in Settings for optimal efficiency.
- **Battery Optimization:**
- — Navigate to Settings > Battery and explore features like Adaptive Power Saving and App Power Management to maximize your device's battery life.
- **One-Handed Mode:**

- Easily enable One-Handed Mode in Settings for a more accessible interface, especially on the larger screen of the Galaxy S24.
- **Camera Quick Launch:**
- Speed up your photo moments by double-pressing the power button to launch the camera instantly, even from the lock screen.
- **DeX Mode for Productivity:**
- Transform your phone into a desktop-like experience using DeX Mode. Simply connect your device to a monitor or TV for an expanded workspace.
- **Bixby Routines:**
- Optimize your device with Bixby Routines by automating tasks based on your usage patterns. Find this gem in Settings and watch your phone adapt to your routine.
- **Gesture Navigation:**
- Embrace gesture navigation for a seamless and immersive experience. Customize gestures in Settings to navigate your device effortlessly.

These Galaxy S24 tips and tricks are your ticket to mastering every aspect of your smartphone. So, buckle up for an enlightening journey through the features that make your Galaxy S24 a powerhouse of convenience and efficiency.

Maximizing Your Galaxy S24 Experience

Unlock the full potential of your Samsung Galaxy S24 with a comprehensive guide on maximizing your smartphone experience. From optimizing settings to exploring advanced features, this journey will elevate your interaction with the Galaxy S24, ensuring that every tap and swipe enhances your daily life.

1. **Personalization for a Tailored Experience:**

- Customize your home screen, app layout, and theme in Settings to create a personalized interface that suits your style.

2. **Biometric Security for Enhanced Protection:**
   - Utilize facial recognition and the ultrasonic fingerprint sensor for advanced security. Fine-tune settings in the Biometrics and Security section to maximize protection.

3. **Optimizing Battery Life:**
   - Navigate to Settings > Battery to explore features like Adaptive Power Saving and App Power Management. Learn how to extend battery life without compromising performance.

4. **Efficient Navigation with Gestures:**
   - Embrace gesture navigation for a smoother and more immersive experience. Customize gestures in Settings to streamline your device navigation.

5. **Utilizing Bixby for Automation:**
   - Explore Bixby Routines in Settings to automate tasks based on your usage patterns. Discover how Bixby adapts to your routine, making your smartphone work for you.

6. **Quick Access with Edge Panels:**
   - Swipe the edge of your screen to access Edge Panels for quick access to apps, contacts, and tools. Customize Edge Panels in Settings to enhance efficiency.

7. **Camera Mastery for Stunning Shots:**
   - Dive into the advanced features of the Quad Ultra Vision Camera System. Explore Director's View, Pro Video mode, and other capabilities to capture cinematic shots.

8. **Streaming and Gaming Excellence:**
   - Leverage the 5G capabilities and GPU Turbocharging feature for seamless streaming and gaming experiences. Maximize visual quality and responsiveness for an immersive entertainment experience.

9. **Advanced Connectivity Options:**

- Explore advanced connectivity features like Super-Fast Charging and Wireless PowerShare. Learn how to use your Galaxy S24 to charge other devices wirelessly.

10. Effortless File Management:
- Simplify file management with features like Quick Share and Nearby Share. Discover how to effortlessly share files between devices.

11. Secure Folder for Confidentiality:
- Create a secure and encrypted space with Secure Folder for confidential files and private content. Learn how to maximize privacy without compromising convenience.

12. Regular Updates for Optimal Performance:
- Keep your Galaxy S24 in top shape by regularly updating software and apps. Explore the benefits of staying current with the latest features and security enhancements.

The guide aims to empower you with the knowledge needed to make the most of your Galaxy S24. From enhancing security to optimizing battery life and exploring advanced features, your smartphone experience is about to reach new heights. Dive in, explore, and maximize your Galaxy S24 to its full potential.

Hidden Features and Shortcuts

Uncover the secrets within your Samsung Galaxy S24 as we delve into a treasure trove of hidden features and shortcuts. This guide is designed to illuminate the less-explored corners of your device, revealing advanced functionalities and time-saving tricks that will elevate your smartphone experience.

Discovering Hidden Gems

1. **Gesture Navigation Mastery:**

- Dive into Settings and explore the Gesture Navigation options. Learn how to seamlessly navigate your device with gestures, making your interaction smoother and more intuitive.

2. **Quick Settings Customization:**
   - Long-press on the Quick Settings icon to access a world of customization. Discover how to tailor your Quick Settings panel for quick access to your most-used features.

3. **Edge Panels for Instant Access:**
   - Swipe the edge of your screen to unveil Edge Panels. Customize these panels in Settings to get instant access to apps, contacts, and tools without interrupting your current screen.

4. **Hidden Camera Features:**
   - Explore the camera app to uncover hidden features. From Pro Video mode to Director's View, learn how to elevate your photography and videography skills with these advanced settings.

5. **Advanced Biometric Security Settings:**
   - Delve into the Biometrics and Security section in Settings to fine-tune your facial recognition and ultrasonic fingerprint sensor settings. Enhance security without sacrificing convenience.

6. **Super Fast Charging Tips:**
   - Understand the nuances of Super Fast Charging. Discover how to optimize charging times and make the most of this powerful feature to get your device up and running quickly.

7. **Maximizing Battery Life:**
   - Navigate through Battery settings to uncover features like Adaptive Power Saving and App Power Management. Learn how to extend your battery life without compromising performance.

8. **DeX Mode for Desktop Experience:**

-   Connect your Galaxy S24 to a monitor or TV and explore the desktop-like experience with DeX Mode. Learn how to leverage this feature for enhanced productivity.

9. **Intelligent Content Recommendations:**
-   Allow your Galaxy S24 to be your content guide. Discover how the device analyzes your usage patterns to offer personalized recommendations for movies, TV shows, and more.

10. **Quick Access to Device Care:**
-   Explore the Device Care feature in Settings to keep your Galaxy S24 in top shape. Learn how to optimize performance, clear storage, and monitor your device's health.

11. **Interactive Air Command:**
-   Hover your S Pen over the screen to activate Air Command. Uncover the plethora of functions and shortcuts available for enhanced productivity with the S Pen.

12. **Camera Quick Launch Shortcut:**
-   Double-press the power button to instantly launch the camera, even from the lock screen. Capture spontaneous moments without missing a beat.

13. **Intuitive Smart Pop-Up View:**
-   Activate Smart Pop-Up View for seamless multitasking. Explore how to use this feature to view and interact with multiple apps simultaneously.

14. **Enhanced File Management:**
-   Discover Quick Share and Nearby Share for effortless file management. Learn how to swiftly share files between devices with these hidden gems.

15. **Secure Folder for Confidentiality:**
-   Create a secure enclave with Secure Folder for confidential files and private content. Uncover how to keep your personal information protected within this encrypted space.

16. **Unveiling Accessibility Features:**

- Dive into Accessibility settings to explore hidden features designed for a personalized and inclusive user experience. Enhance the accessibility of your device to suit your needs.

Unlock the potential of your Galaxy S24 by exploring these hidden features and shortcuts. This guide is your roadmap to a more enriched and efficient smartphone experience. Navigate with confidence, customize with ease, and make your Galaxy S24 truly yours.

Customization Options for Personalized Usage

Elevate your Samsung Galaxy S24 experience by embracing a world of customization options that cater to your unique preferences. In this comprehensive guide, we'll navigate through the rich array of features and settings that allow you to tailor your device to suit your style, making every interaction with your Galaxy S24 a truly personalized and enjoyable experience.

a. **Home Screen Customization:**
   - Long-press on the home screen to access customization options. Learn how to resize widgets, change wallpapers, and organize your apps for a personalized and aesthetically pleasing home screen.

b. **Themes and Icons:**
   - Dive into Themes in Settings to explore a variety of visual styles for your device. Customize your icons, wallpapers, and system-wide color schemes to reflect your personality.

c. **Dynamic Lock Screen:**
   - Explore Dynamic Lock Screen options in Settings to keep your lock screen fresh and engaging. Learn how to set up dynamic wallpapers that change throughout the day.

d. **Always On Display Personalization:**

-   Customize your Always on Display in Settings. Discover how to choose clock styles, add personal signatures, and display useful information without unlocking your device.

e. Edge Lighting Effects:

-   Activate Edge Lighting for visually stunning notifications. Customize the lighting effects and colors in Settings to add a personal touch to your device's notifications.

f. Quick Settings Customization:

-   Long-press on the Quick Settings icon to access customization options. Rearrange and add or remove quick settings tiles to streamline your device's functionality.

g. Font and Text Customization:

-   Explore Font and Screen Zoom options in Settings for personalized text styles and sizes. Tailor the display to ensure comfortable reading and a visually appealing interface.

h. Navigation Bar and Gestures:

-   Choose between traditional navigation buttons or gestures in Settings. Experiment with gesture navigation for a more immersive and fluid device interaction.

i. Biometric Security Customization:

-   Fine-tune facial recognition and the ultrasonic fingerprint sensor settings in Biometrics and Security. Optimize security features to align with your preferences.

j. Bixby Routines for Automated Customization:

-   Set up Bixby Routines in Settings for automated customization based on your usage patterns. Discover how your Galaxy S24 adapts to your routine, enhancing efficiency and convenience.

k. Advanced Display Settings:

-   Explore advanced display settings in Settings > Display. Adjust color balance, screen mode, and blue light filter to create a display experience tailored to your liking.

l. Sound and Vibration Personalization:

- Customize sound and vibration settings in Sound and Vibration settings. Choose ringtones, notification sounds, and vibration patterns that resonate with your preferences.

m. S Pen Settings and Features:
- If you have an S Pen, explore the settings and features specific to this accessory. Learn how to use Air Command, create notes, and unlock additional capabilities for enhanced productivity.

n. App Icon Badges and Notifications:
- Tailor app icon badges and notification settings in Settings > Notifications. Optimize how you receive and interact with notifications for a clutter-free experience.

o. Secure Folder for Private Customization:
- Customize a private space within your device using Secure Folder. Personalize this encrypted space with apps, files, and content that require an extra layer of security.

p. Scheduled Dark Mode:
- Set up Scheduled Dark Mode in Display settings to automatically switch between light and dark modes based on your preferred time. Customize your device's appearance for different lighting conditions.

q. Accessibility Customization:
- Explore Accessibility settings for a personalized and inclusive experience. Adjust settings such as font size, magnification gestures, and more to cater to your specific needs.

r. Regularly Update Wallpaper and Themes:
- Keep your device's look fresh by regularly updating wallpapers and themes. Explore new themes and wallpapers to refresh your device's appearance.

This guide empowers you to unlock the full potential of customization on your Galaxy S24. Whether it's visual aesthetics, functionality, or security, your device can be tailored to align perfectly with your preferences. Dive into the settings, experiment with different options, and craft a Galaxy S24 experience that is uniquely yours.

CHAPTER ELEVEN

TROUBLESHOOTING AND FAQS

Dive into the world of tech wizardry with Galaxy S24 Troubleshooting—a systematic guide that transforms problem-solving into an art form. Unravel the mysteries of malfunction, charting a course from symptoms to solutions. Just like a detective cracking a case, the first step is to decode the enigma—what are the symptoms? Where does it strike? When does the glitch make its grand entrance? Under what cosmic conditions does it unfold? Get ready to be your smartphone's superhero, armed with the power of problem-solving prowess. the realm of troubleshooting, where the art of problem-solving transforms into a meticulous dance of logic and systematic exploration. This intricate process is a beacon of hope when products or processes falter, an endeavor to resurrect the operational essence of your machine or system.

At its core, troubleshooting is akin to detective work, a methodical journey to unearth the source of a problem and engineer its resolution. The process is a tapestry of logical steps, each woven with the intention of not just fixing the issue but breathing life back into the product or process. The troubleshooter's journey commences with the identification of symptoms—a detailed mapping of the anomalies that disrupt the seamless operation. With this diagnostic groundwork laid, the troubleshooter embarks on a journey of elimination, systematically ruling out potential causes until the elusive culprit is unmasked. Every step is a delicate dance between deduction and experimentation, an intricate web of decisions leading to the most likely cause. As the troubleshooter narrows down the possibilities, the true artistry lies in confirming that the proposed solution is not just a fix but a resurrection—an alchemical transformation that restores the product or process to its intended state of operational grace. In this world of troubleshooting, each challenge becomes a canvas, and every solution is a stroke of mastery, ensuring that the intricate machinery of your device or system hums with vitality once more. Welcome to the symphony of systematic problem-solving, where each troubleshooter is a maestro orchestrating the restoration of operational harmony.

Galaxy S24 FAQs—an illuminating guide designed to unravel the mysteries, demystify the perplexing, and provide clarity amidst the technological cosmos. From the most common queries to the intricate curiosities, this FAQ adventure is your compass in navigating the vast universe of your Samsung Galaxy S24. Get ready to dive into a constellation of knowledge, where every question finds its stellar answer.

Common Issues and Solutions

a. **Battery Woes**
- **Issue:** Rapid battery drains or inconsistent charging.
- **Solution:** Investigate battery usage in settings, optimize background apps, and consider recalibrating the battery. Check for rogue apps consuming power excessively.

b. **Connectivity Challenges:**
- **Issue:** Wi-Fi or mobile data connectivity issues.
- **Solution:** Toggle airplane mode, reset network settings, or forget and rejoin Wi-Fi networks. Ensure mobile data and data-saving settings are appropriately configured.

c. **App Glitches:**
- **Issue:** Apps crashing or freezing.
- **Solution:** Update apps regularly, clear app cache, and consider reinstalling problematic apps. Check for compatibility issues with the latest software update.

d. **Slow Performance:**

- **Issue:** Lag or slowdowns in device performance.
- **Solution:** Close unnecessary background apps, optimize device storage, and consider a factory reset if the issue persists. Ensure your device has the latest software updates.

e. **Overheating Concerns:**
- **Issue:** Device heating up during usage.
- **Solution:** Check for resource-intensive apps, avoid prolonged usage in direct sunlight, and remove unnecessary covers or cases. Ensure your device is running the latest software version.

f. **Camera Quirks:**
- **Issue:** Camera not focusing, blurry images, or app crashes.
- **Solution:** Clean the camera lens, ensure the camera app is updated, and troubleshoot using safe mode to rule out third-party app interference.

g. **Storage Struggles:**
- **Issue:** Insufficient storage warnings or difficulties managing files.
- **Solution:** Delete unnecessary files, clear app cache, and consider transferring media to external storage. Utilize Smart Storage features for automated management.

h. **Biometric Blues:**
- **Issue:** Face recognition or fingerprint sensor malfunctions.
- **Solution:** Re-register biometric data, ensure the sensors are clean, and troubleshoot in safe mode to identify potential conflicts with third-party apps.

i. **Software Quandaries:**
- **Issue:** Software glitches or unexpected behaviors.
- **Solution:** Keep your device updated with the latest software releases, perform regular reboots, and consider a factory reset if persistent issues arise.

j. **Security Conundrums:**
- **Issue:** Authentication or security concerns.

- **Solution:** Update security settings, ensure your device is protected with a secure password, and consider reviewing app permissions for enhanced security.
k. **Sound and Audio Issues:**
- **Issue:** Distorted audio, low volume, or connectivity problems with Bluetooth devices.
- **Solution:** Check audio settings, clear Bluetooth cache, and ensure your device is connected to the latest software version.
l. **Screen Glitches:**
- **Issue:** Display anomalies, touch screen issues, or flickering.
- **Solution:** Adjust display settings, perform a screen calibration, and troubleshoot in safe mode to identify potential third-party app interference.
m. **Frequent Updates:**
- **Issue:** Frequent notifications for software updates.
- **Solution:** Embrace regular updates as they often bring improvements, bug fixes, and enhanced features. Set up automatic updates for convenience.
n. **Factory Reset Considerations:**
- **Issue:** Persistent issues with no resolution.
- **Solution:** As a last resort, perform a factory reset. Ensure to back up essential data before proceeding.

As you navigate the Galaxy S24 cosmos, these solutions serve as your reliable companions, guiding you through the vast universe of common issues. May your smartphone journey be filled with seamless experiences and boundless exploration.

Troubleshooting Connectivity Problems

Navigating the interconnected galaxy of your Samsung Galaxy S24 can sometimes encounter turbulence in the form of connectivity issues. Fear not, intrepid explorer, for this guide is your beacon through the cosmic expanse of troubleshooting. Let's embark on a journey to unravel and resolve connectivity challenges, ensuring your smartphone experience remains seamlessly connected.

1. Wi-Fi Woes:

Symptoms:

- Unable to connect to Wi-Fi networks.
- Intermittent disconnections.

Troubleshooting Steps:

- Toggle Wi-Fi off and on.
- Forget and reconnect to the network.
- Reset network settings in device settings.
- Update router firmware.
- Check for interference from other electronic devices.

2. Mobile Data Dilemmas:

Symptoms:

- Inconsistent mobile data connection.
- Slow data speeds.

Troubleshooting Steps:

- Enable and disable airplane mode.
- Check for data restrictions in device settings.
- Reset network settings.
- Contact your carrier for potential network issues.
- Ensure mobile data is enabled in device settings.

3. Bluetooth Blues:

Symptoms:

- Difficulty connecting to Bluetooth devices.
- Frequent disconnections.

Troubleshooting Steps:

- Toggle Bluetooth off and on.
- Forget and re-pair Bluetooth devices.
- Clear Bluetooth cache in device settings.
- Ensure the devices are within the Bluetooth range.
- Check for software updates on connected devices.

4. GPS Glitches:

Symptoms:

- Inaccurate location information.
- Difficulty acquiring GPS signal.

Troubleshooting Steps:

- Enable and disable location services.
- Ensure GPS is set to high accuracy in device settings.
- Update Google Maps or any GPS-dependent apps.
- Calibrate the compass in device settings.
- Restart the device for a fresh GPS connection.

5. Network-Related Nuisances:

Symptoms:

- Unstable network connection.
- Calls or texts not going through.

Troubleshooting Steps:

- Check for carrier outages in your area.
- Ensure your SIM card is properly inserted.
- Reset network settings.
- Contact your carrier for assistance.
- Verify call and message blocking settings.

6. Hotspot Hassles:

Symptoms:

- Issues with creating or connecting to a mobile hotspot.

Troubleshooting Steps:

- Verify that mobile data is enabled.
- Reset network settings.
- Change hotspot settings, including password and security.
- Ensure the connected device is within the hotspot range.
- Update the device's hotspot firmware.

7. Software Snags:

Symptoms:

- Connectivity issues after a recent software update.
- Random connection drops.

Troubleshooting Steps:

- Check for the latest software updates.
- Clear cache partition in recovery mode.
- Consider a factory reset if issues persist.
- Contact Samsung Support for further assistance.

8. Advanced Network Settings:

Symptoms:

- Advanced network settings causing problems.

Troubleshooting Steps:

- Disable advanced network settings temporarily.
- Monitor for improvements.
- Re-enable settings selectively if needed.

9. Professional Help:

If all else fails, consider reaching out to Samsung Support or your carrier for professional assistance. They can provide specific guidance based on your device's unique situation.

As you embark on this connectivity troubleshooting journey, may your Galaxy S24 find its celestial alignment, and may your digital travels be marked by uninterrupted connectivity.

Frequently Asked Questions about the Galaxy S24

Galaxy of curiosity—the realm of Frequently Asked Questions about your Samsung Galaxy S24. In this guide, we'll embark on a journey to demystify the queries that often orbit the minds of users. Get ready to uncover insights, troubleshoot uncertainties, and enhance your understanding of the stellar device in your hands.

1. **Q:** How do I maximize battery life on my Galaxy S24?

A: To optimize battery life, consider adjusting screen brightness, managing background apps, and enabling power-saving modes. Regularly updating your device and avoiding extreme temperatures can also contribute to prolonged battery health.

2. **Q:** How can I customize my home screen on the Galaxy S24?

A: Long-press on the home screen to access customization options. You can resize widgets, change wallpapers, and organize apps for a personalized and aesthetically pleasing home screen.

3. **Q:** What should I do if my Galaxy S24 is overheating?

A: Overheating may be caused by resource-intensive apps or environmental factors. Close unnecessary apps, avoid direct sunlight, and remove unnecessary covers. Ensure your device is running the latest software version.

4. **Q**: How do I troubleshoot connectivity issues on my Galaxy S24?

A: Troubleshoot connectivity challenges by toggling Wi-Fi or mobile data off and on, resetting network settings, and checking for software updates. Specific steps depend on the type of connectivity issue you're facing.

5. **Q:** Can I expand storage on the Galaxy S24?

A: While the Galaxy S24 comes with ample internal storage, you can expand it using a microSD card. Insert a compatible card to enjoy additional space for photos, videos, and apps.

6. **Q:** What's the best way to clean the camera lens on my Galaxy S24?

A: Use a microfiber cloth to gently wipe the camera lens. Avoid abrasive materials that may scratch the lens. Cleaning the lens ensures clear and crisp photos.

7. **Q:** How do I enable facial recognition on my Galaxy S24?

A: Navigate to Settings > Biometrics and Security > Face Recognition. Follow the on-screen instructions to register your face. Ensure you're in a well-lit environment during the setup process.

8. **Q:** Can I use the Galaxy S24 while charging?

A: Yes, you can use your Galaxy S24 while charging. However, using resource-intensive apps may slow down the charging process. It's recommended to use the provided charger and cable for optimal charging speed.

9. **Q:** What's the best way to protect my Galaxy S24 from malware?

A: Keep your device updated with the latest security patches and use reputable antivirus apps. Avoid downloading apps from unofficial sources and be cautious with unknown links.

10. **Q:** How do I transfer data from my old device to the Galaxy S24?

A: Use the Samsung Smart Switch app to transfer data seamlessly. The app supports various transfer methods, including a cable connection, wireless transfer, and even transferring from an iPhone.

11. **Q:** Can I use wireless charging with my Galaxy S24?

A: Yes, the Galaxy S24 supports wireless charging. You can use compatible wireless chargers to charge your device conveniently.

12. **Q:** How do I enable Dark Mode on my Galaxy S24?

A: Navigate to Settings > Display > Dark mode. You can choose to enable Dark Mode all the time or schedule it based on your preferences.

13. **Q:** Can I take underwater photos with my Galaxy S24?

A: While the Galaxy S24 is water-resistant, it's not designed for extended underwater use. It's recommended to avoid submerging the device for prolonged periods. However, it can handle accidental splashes and brief exposure to water.

14. **Q:** How often should I update my Galaxy S24?

A: Regularly updating your device ensures you have the latest features, security patches, and bug fixes. Set up automatic updates or check for updates manually in Settings.

15. **Q:** What do I do if my Galaxy S24 freezes or becomes unresponsive?

A: Perform a soft reset by holding down the power and volume down buttons simultaneously for about 10 seconds. If the issue persists, consider a factory reset after backing up your data.

16. **Q:** Can I customize the Edge Panels on my Galaxy S24?

A: Yes, you can customize Edge Panels by going to Settings > Display > Edge screen. Adjust the order of panels, download new ones, and customize their appearance to suit your preferences.

17. **Q:** How do I access the Secure Folder on my Galaxy S24?

A: Secure Folder provides an encrypted space for sensitive data. Access it through the Apps screen or the Quick Panel. Follow the on-screen instructions to set up and customize your Secure Folder.

18. **Q:** What features does the S Pen offer on the Galaxy S24?

A: If your device supports the S Pen, you can use it for various functions, including Air Command, creating notes, and drawing. Explore S Pen settings in the device's settings menu for customization options.

19. **Q:** Can I use third-party accessories with my Galaxy S24?

A: While many third-party accessories are compatible, it's recommended to use official Samsung accessories for optimal performance and to avoid potential compatibility issues.

20. **Q:** How do I enable the Super Steady video mode on my Galaxy S24?

A: Open the Camera app, navigate to Video mode, and select Super Steady from the shooting modes. This feature enhances video stabilization for smoother recording.

This Galaxy S24 FAQs aims to equip you with knowledge, troubleshooting tips, and insights to make your smartphone journey as seamless as possible. For further assistance, consult the Samsung Support team or explore the vibrant community of Galaxy users. Happy exploring.

CONCLUSION

As we culminate our exploration into the intricate world of the Samsung Galaxy S24, it is a moment to contemplate the multifaceted journey through its revolutionary features, design marvels, and technological prowess. Beyond being a mere smartphone, the Galaxy S24 serves as a testament to human ingenuity and an unwavering commitment to excellence in the realm of mobile technology. The moment Galaxy S24 rests in your hands, its ergonomic design and premium build materials redefine the very essence of sophistication. Meticulously crafted aesthetics, complemented by a color palette inspired by both nature and contemporary trends, elevate this device into an aesthetic marvel. The visual odyssey commences with the immersive Infinity-O Dynamic AMOLED display, a technological masterpiece transcending the boundaries of visual brilliance. This meticulously engineered display technology reshapes your perception of content, rendering vibrant multimedia, revealing intricate details in photos, and delivering seamless transitions in your favorite applications. The Quad Ultra Vision Camera System, spearheaded by the formidable 108MP main sensor, empowers every shot with an unparalleled level of detail. AI-driven enhancements push the boundaries of your photography experience, while NightVision technology ensures your low-light captures shine with unprecedented clarity. At the core of the Galaxy S24 lies the Exynos 7nm+ Octa-Core Processor, a powerhouse not only ensuring efficiency and speed but also paving the way for GPU Turbocharging, transforming gaming into an immersive spectacle. The device sets new benchmarks in performance, effortlessly handling the demands of modern applications and games.

Seamless connectivity for the modern user is not just a promise; it's a reality. The Galaxy S24 embraces the 5G revolution, ensuring that your streaming, gaming, and communication experiences are not just fast but future-proofed for the evolving digital landscape. Battery longevity and charging innovations are a testament to Samsung's commitment to user convenience. Adaptive Power Saving Mode, coupled with AI-driven optimization, ensures your device intelligently adapts to usage patterns, maximizing battery life. In the ever-evolving digital landscape, the Galaxy S24 stands tall with its Biometric Authentication, Ultrasonic Fingerprint Sensor, and the impregnable fortress of the Samsung Knox Security Platform. Privacy and data protection measures are not mere features but a promise to safeguard your digital identity. The Galaxy S24 transcends being just a smartphone; it transforms into your personal entertainment hub. Dolby Atmos Audio Technology delivers immersive sound, while expanded storage capacity ensures that your cinematic experiences are not bound by limits. It becomes a portal of limitless possibilities for entertainment on the go.

As we embark on the final leg of our journey, delve into a guide that goes beyond the ordinary—the realm of tips, tricks, troubleshooting, and FAQs. Discover the hidden features, shortcuts, and customization options that elevate your Galaxy S24 experience from great to extraordinary. Wrapping up this odyssey through the Samsung Galaxy S24, remember that this device is more than the sum of its parts. It's an embodiment of innovation, a conduit for your creativity, and a companion in your digital endeavors. May your journey with the Galaxy S24 be filled with discovery, seamless connectivity, and endless possibilities. Safe travels in the galaxy of innovation.